Art Making & Studio Spaces

Green Altar, Laurie Zuckerman

QUARRY

First published in the United States of America by
Quarry Books, a member of
Quayside Publishing Group
100 Cummings Center
Suite 406-L
Beverly, Massachusetts 01915-6101
Telephone: (978) 282-9590
Fax: (978) 283-2742
www.quarrybooks.com
Visit www.Craftside.Typepad.com for a behind-the-scenes peek at our crafty world!

Library of Congress Cataloging-in-Publication Data

Perrella, Lynne.
  Art making and studio spaces : unleash your inner artist : an intimate look at 31 creative workspaces / Lynne Perrella.
       p. cm.
  Includes index.
  ISBN-13: 978-1-59253-539-2
  ISBN-10: 1-59253-539-9
  1. Artists' studios. I. Title.
  N8520.P48 2010
  702.8--dc22

                                                              2009026732
                                                              CIP

ISBN-13: 978-1-59253-539-2
ISBN-10: 1-59253-539-9

10 9 8 7 6 5 4 3 2 1

Design: Laura H. Couallier, Laura Herrmann Design
Photography: Sarah Blodgett
Art direction: Lynne Perrella, with the following exceptions: pages 1 and 176: Laurie Zuckerman; pages 32–35: Michelle Ward; pages 36–43: Pam Sussman; pages 44–47: Studio Rossi, Inc.; pages 48–49: Ellen Kochansky; pages 74–77: Tracy V. Moore; pages 82–87: Keith LoBue; pages 88–91: Tobin Rogers; page 96: Steven Sorman; pages 150–155: Michael deMeng; pages 156–165: Judy Wilkenfeld
Artwork for visual essays, pages 22–25, 32–35, 48–49, 74–77: Lynne Perrella

Printed in Singapore

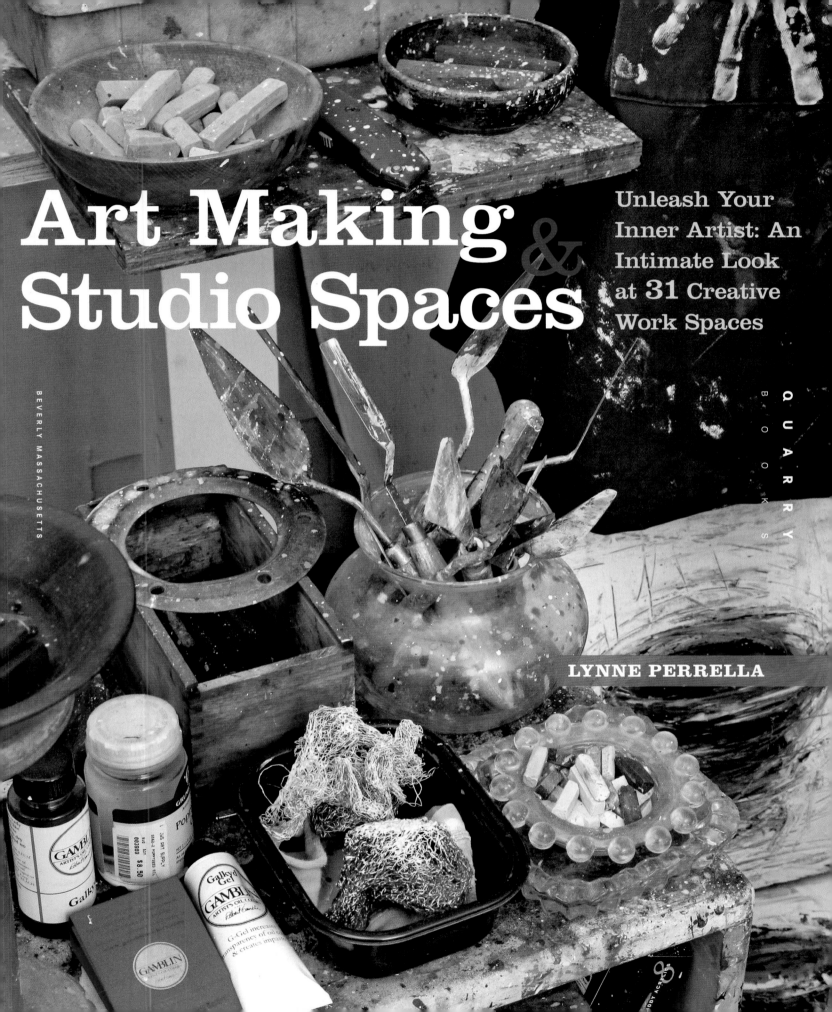

Art Making & Studio Spaces

Unleash Your Inner Artist: An Intimate Look at **31** Creative Work Spaces

BEVERLY MASSACHUSETTS

QUARRY BOOKS

LYNNE PERRELLA

CONTENTS

Terri Moore's sketchbook sits amid an array of her favorite things: nests, pods, treasured amulets, feathers, a box of vintage thread, a phonograph arm, and more.

INTRODUCTION

Several years ago, I attended a definitive exhibition of the lifelong spectrum of Jackson Pollock's work at the Museum of Modern Art in New York City. For years, I had been getting by with a "Cliff notes" cursory knowledge of Pollock, and I looked forward to immersing myself in the chronologically arranged exhibit. Walking the galleries, I tracked his early development and influences, followed by the eventual rumblings that produced his well-known, culture-bending abstract paintings. It was a rewarding and stimulating day. In a dimly lit final gallery, I ducked through a curious low doorway and found myself *inside* Pollock's studio. In a stroke of genius, the museum had installed a replica of Pollock's small, rustic painting barn/studio in Springs, New York. I was surrounded by rough-sawn wooden walls, ceiling and floorboards encrusted with spontaneous splatters of paint, reminders of his definitive "poured" paintings. The distinctive aroma of solvents, paints, and pigments lingered, along with the familiar, nostalgic smell of household tools and gardening equipment. It was an intimate space that provoked looks of wonder and hushed reflections from visitors as they considered the rare opportunity to pay a visit, no matter how unexpected, to Jackson Pollock's studio. On that long-ago afternoon, the idea for this book was born.

Unlike other rooms, studios defy the usual rules of form and function. Never truly "finished" or static, these work spaces are available, elastic, and open for business, while remaining intensely private and personal. When I asked

The perfect brush, the ideal tool ... all await the confident hand of Steven Sorman in his printmaking studio in Columbia County, New York.

artists to define or describe their studios, I received a highly varied list of characterizations: "It's my favorite place"; "It's my laboratory"; "It's the epicenter for all my ideas, as well as all my junk"; "It's my retreat, my solace"; "It's my work room—where I never have to clean up."

This remarkable, creative group of artists has thrown open the doors, windows, and drawers of their studios and welcomed us inside. From tiny pocket studios behind closed doors to sprawling spaces that defy boundaries and sometimes edge into the great outdoors; from calm, meticulous, well-ordered ateliers designed to pass the white-glove test to riotous, overflowing work rooms awash in tangled power tools, sliding piles of rusted art fodder, and paint palettes that look more like ashtrays; from artfully arranged bibelots and artifacts to hasty pencil scrawls and reminders written on a nearby wall—it's all here. Thankfully, there is no "wrong way" to conceive and arrange a studio, and many of these artists admit that their spaces just sort of, well, "happened."

I'm reminded of an apt quote from our spirit guide for this adventure, Jackson Pollock. On the back of a photo of himself in his studio, he scrawled, "Organic intensity— Energy—and motion made visible—memories arrested in space—human needs and motives—acceptance."

Unique and distinctive as its inhabitant and personal as a signature, each studio awaits. The tour begins *now*.

Lynne Perrella

W elcome to my studio, where sometimes the music comes on before the lights.

Depending on my mood, I listen to medieval chants on the CD player or walk over to the vintage jukebox and hit the selector buttons for some Golden Oldies. Bright sunlight streams into the room by day; in the evening, I readjust the lighting with lamps and maybe even some party lights. Colorful, cluttered, and undeniably cheerful, the room is defined by my favorite things: a curvaceous, rustic Adirondack rocking chair, my favorite photos of friends and family, and fresh flowers. The walls are a warm, welcoming shade of melon, but the room gets its strongest burst of color from the countless books that line almost every wall and a growing collection of vivid, multiethnic folk-art personas. These figures, the colorful guardians of the studio, inspire me and remind me of the community of artisans from all cultures who take their joy in "just making things."

Years ago, I decided that "work room" was the ideal description for my studio, because the term provides some strong cover for the occasional eruptions of chaos and disorder that are inevitable as I work on several projects at once. Large, white, metal flat files, left over from my previous life as a commercial artist, provide storage solutions and organization, but I am just as likely to "start a new pile" of art supplies while I am brainstorming a new idea. Although I sometimes favor the "everything out in the open" approach, I am always searching for more vintage wooden storage cabinets, especially defunct library or type-shop pieces with endless drawers.

After years of working at a conventional tilt-top artist's drawing board with clip-on lamps, I treated myself to a massive, vintage oak drafting table. Not only is it more spacious and conducive, it's large enough for a row of handsome rustic wooden tool carriers and imprinted cigar boxes that hold my supplies. Seymour, the cat, my sleek, black furry studio manager, commands a place on my desk, near the window, and keeps watch.

Nearby is a stack of quotation dictionaries that provide instant word play, and a sheaf of black construction paper is always at the ready if I need a brain tickling exercise to get me started. My bulletin board—full of favorite images, photos, quotes, news clippings and souvenirs—provides ever-changing paper compost, and it is the first place I go when I want a quick blast of visual stimulation.

Oscar Wilde stated that he could resist anything but temptation, and I can never resist the temptation to bring home another stack of books. A comparatively harmless passion, my continuing dilemma is figuring out where to put all the volumes that fill the bookcases and then become "overflow." Research is one of my favorite aspects of any project, so my studio is as much a reading room as a place for creating, with comfortable spots to pull up a chair and investigate a new idea. Books on history of costume, art history, puppetry and theatrical design, and store-window display top my list; plus, a couple of shelves are devoted to the writings by and about Jack Kerouac. My art journals have their own special place, along with written diaries and idea notebooks.

A back room, notoriously known as "the prop room," has floor-to-ceiling shelves for mixed-media supplies and spontaneous collections. Anything that might come in handy for a collage, assemblage, art doll, or gift wrap idea ends up there.

My studio is a colorful cocoon, where I can create any mood I want by adjusting the lights, turning the music up or down, pulling out my favorite materials for making art, and beginning the exploration process. Not created according to any master plan with graph paper and tape measure, this area, which commands the ground level of our home, has happened over many years and has morphed according to my interests and fascinations.

Through it all, it has become an organic reflection of who I am and why I look forward to going to my studio every day. ⦿

"My current studio reminds me of the little bedroom I had growing up. In a way, it was my 'first' studio, and it always overflowed with mad experiments, midnight projects, endless tapping on the typewriter, and sliding piles of papers and bits of cardboard. Some things never change!"

— **LYNNE PERRELLA**

ORIENTATION
Maximalism. Without Apology.
GPS 40.422078° latitude
−105.101381° longitude

Size doesn't matter. As proof, Lisa Hoffman recalls some of her previous studios and admits that they were postage stamp–sized. Now that she has a generous, expansive studio in the lower level of her home, she still claims that square footage is not a criteria: "Very good work comes from within," she says. And though this sentiment obviously comes from the heart, her current studio allows her leeway to bring in a whole host of feel-good elements that keep her visually stimulated and completely at home.

"I am a collector by nature and have filled my space with things that excite, inspire, and evoke my creative energy," Lisa says. "I keep adding lights everywhere I can: table lamps, work lights, and holiday lights in my fireplace for illumination-without-pollution. A family of birds that bring music and joy, and my two dogs nearby at all times. I like to keep it fun."

LISA HOFFMAN

In a colorful corner of the studio, floor-to-ceiling wooden shelves hold a vast selection of rubber stamps, paints, and solvents, and the foreground overflows with large Day of the Dead papier mâché skulls and rolls of vibrant decorative papers stuck into large, colorful vases. Strands of party lights provide additional lighting, proving there is a fine line between work and play.

Colorful bulletin boards appear throughout the space; each is constantly updated with new photos, graphics, postcards, and photos of friends and family. Lisa rotates the visuals and adds new layers of idea fodder, so everything feels "new but familiar." Regardless of her mindset, the studio provides the ideal environment for creativity. "If I'm in a Forward-Go mode, it gives me the push I need. If I am feeling depleted, I can go in there to revive and replenish. Without guilt."

"I love the position of my studio worktables. The large L-shape allows me to use one section as a work space, while the other holds all my supplies. Elevating the work desk on PVC pipes brings it up to a comfortable height, so I can stand and work … and the tables are positioned to face the windows. Bring in the view! I love to have guests pull up a stool and stay. After all, it's one of my favorite places, so it's a comfortable space for sharing with close friends."

Because Lisa works on large pieces that incorporate paint, having space and light becomes increasingly important. Although she gives a lot of thought to "weeding out" and streamlining her studio, she also laughingly admits to having a penchant for surrounding herself with all her favorite "stuff." "There goes the entire notion of streamlined!"

"I love to see personal artifacts in a studio… things that identify and reveal the artist's interior landscape. My own studio is brimming with items that are so personal I call them 'external tattoos.'"

— LISA HOFFMAN

LISA HOFFMAN

Shelves hold whimsical armies of designer vinyl toys, including some small ceramic figures that she uses in mixed-media assemblages, when she can bear to part with them. Things she uses frequently, her favorite tools and supplies, are displayed in creative ways to make the art-making process more enjoyable and personal. Paintbrushes are corralled in vases, buckets, and glass jars. Pliers and wire cutters are kept in old wooden sugar molds. Tubes of paint are arrayed in vintage colorful ceramic bowls and vessels. Decorative papers are arranged on the rungs of old wooden ladders, everything visible at a glance.

In a quiet corner, a still life appears on the hearth of the stone fireplace. Saved shards of a mirror owned by Lisa's great grandmother, devotional votive candles from Santa Fe, a postcard of the Black Madonna, silk roses, sea shells, a tangle of white holiday lights, and other significant found objects comprise a studio shrine. Music plays, and birdsong is heard, along with an occasional enthusiastic yelp from one of the white dogs. Tea is brewing.

"My studio is a warm, cozy, and inspiring place for me," says Lisa. "It provides me with a safe space for experimentation. It's all here. No excuses." ◐

ORIENTATION
Caravan DeLuxe
GPS 36.4047047° latitude
−105.584812° longitude

If, indeed, one needs an excuse to buy a vintage 1960 Land Yacht Airstream trailer, Lyn Beiler had the perfect rationale: "My creative endeavors and mixed-media art supplies were spilling over into all areas of our tiny, old adobe home."

A long-time aficionado of the classic aluminum-clad recreational vehicles originally marketed in the 1930s, Lyn found a "For Sale" ad in her local newspaper. Buying the Airstream not only fulfilled a dream of owning her own trailer, it provided an added benefit: "Practically overnight, I had a studio of my own," Lyn says.

Although trailers evoke images of wanderlust and spontaneous travels, Lyn's has been given a permanent home, parked behind her authentic, New-Mexico-style adobe house in Taos. Surrounded by sturdy bales of fresh hay, the studio trailer is the focal point in a backyard that has become a lively barnyard, complete with sheep, kittens, innumerable chickens, and at least one feisty rooster.

The Airstream's rounded body, designed to be aerodynamic and functional, is a work of art on its own, but Lyn's decorative additions have added both heart and soul to the interior. Every inch of the trailer is maximized, including the use of the refrigerator and oven as places to stash works of art in progress when other projects take precedence. Her initial plan was to convert the two sleeping bunks to storage areas, but she soon realized the value of having a ready-made reading nook, complete with built-in reading lamp, and a place in which to curl up for an afternoon nap or a little daydreaming.

Lyn frequently admires her studio and the surrounding chorus of lively animal friends while having a meditative soak in a clawfoot tub, in a bathroom full of vintage fixtures. She values the mobility of carrying works of art in progress from the trailer to the house, setting up a painting or journal page on a sideboard or window sill to ponder over it.

A collection of vintage suitcases, a perfect reminder of the vacation-like atmosphere of the travel trailer, is helpful for hauling gesso and paints into the house to work near a roaring fire in the kiva fireplace and is useful as storage. Every part of her environment inspires her and provides a distinctive mood for creating or sparring with new ideas. A childhood habit of claiming a solitary place to curl up and call her own persists, and the trailer provides Lyn with a private sanctuary.

LYN BLEILER

"Privacy and being removed from distractions such as the phone, fax, and knocks on the front door are paramount. I like to feel I am entering a womb-like space that is my own little world, and the Airstream provides all of that and more."

— LYN BLEILER

Lyn describes entering her trailer studio and sensing a "homecoming aspect," acknowledging that her biggest challenge is focusing on a single project at a time. Even to visitors, the trailer exudes the welcoming playful mood of a party caravan, and the décor reflects the owner's feminine side. Vintage floral and cowgirl-themed bark cloth in shades of dusty pink and rose are used for drapes and upholstery, festive party lights stretch in bright twinkling strands across the interior, and starlet publicity photos from the '40s provide a savvy wink and a grin. Ongoing collections of vintage wallpapers from the '40s and '50s are gradually transforming the interior walls, and favorite pieces of prized California pottery underline a "surrounded-by-treasures" mood, affirming Lyn's observance that "it's a 'chicks-only' zone."

Has having her own studio—even one as unique as the Airstream—unleashed her creative license?

"Even when I am away, knowing the studio is there waiting brings me pleasure," Lyn says. She describes her usual mood in the studio as "youthful, inspired, playful, and free," her words proof of the supportive and encouraging atmosphere she has created in this unique environment.

The old trailer seems to hold the vibes of previous journeys, and unexpected bursts of travel lust just seem to happen. Lyn recalls pulling the homemade drapes closed one cold winter day and visualizing the trailer/studio moving through the desert, heading for sunny California—with all the comforts of home. ◉

A card posted near the entry door reads: "I live in my own little world. But it's okay. Everyone knows me here." The quiet sounds of animals outside the trailer on a summer day provide a reminder of the natural surroundings, and "on several occasions one of our sheep has nudged the screen door open and sauntered right in."

Who doesn't love an "upgrade"? Monica's former studio, before the family devised a home renovation that nearly doubled their living space, was a humble uninsulated back porch that also functioned as a mud room, seasonal clothing storage area, and laundry room. Factor in Monica's admitted "galloping abundance" of mixed-media supplies and found objects, and a creative landfill was inevitable. Now, the entry door, emblazoned with a brass numeral 3, opens to a rectangular, light-filled work area, full of significant treasures.

Why the number three? To Monica, it represents creative activity and symbolizes the formation of ideas. When a recent visitor to the studio asked, "How did you get all this *stuff*?," the question caused Monica to reflect, and she provided the cheerful and knowing answer: "Over a lifetime, of course!" The compact studio provides visual stimulation at all turns, from a rollicking pinboard full of postcards, quotes, and quips to the unexpected fascination of a small, portable document carrier bursting with "idea files" labeled with colored markers.

**WORKING OFF THE GRID...
ONE OF MONICA'S UNIQUE
HEART ASSEMBLAGES,
COVERED IN SMALL SQUARES
OF TIN, LICENSE PLATES,
METAL ODDITIES, AND MORE.**

A visit to her studio is a bit like learning Monica's family history; she surrounds herself with furnishings and objects that hold a longtime fascination and meaning for her. The drawers of a childhood dresser, painted and repainted over time, are full of art supplies and tools, and the top is an area for staging an ever-changing tableau. Today, it displays a vintage doll's wardrobe closet, with crackled paint and Bakelite knobs, holding Monica's sketchbooks, as well as a wooden clock case that shelters small figures and art dolls from many cultures—her self-described "Invincible Women Shrine." They catch the morning light from the "three-in-a-row" windows that overlook a perennial garden and outdoor bench and provide Monica with her wished-for "room with a view." Because this mixed-media artist is also a master gardener, she is able to create interior *and* exterior beauty and enjoy both.

"I like a sun drenched space," Monica says. The freshly painted cantaloupe-colored walls create a welcoming cocoon and a sumptuous backdrop for her artwork and the shelves of supplies and files. She prefers to have art materials visually accessible (a challenge for an artist who literally works with almost every material imaginable): vintage cast-iron muffin tins hold a series of small items, and transparent plastic storage containers and boxes keep the ever-growing banquet of possibilities in view.

Assemblage, Monica Riffe

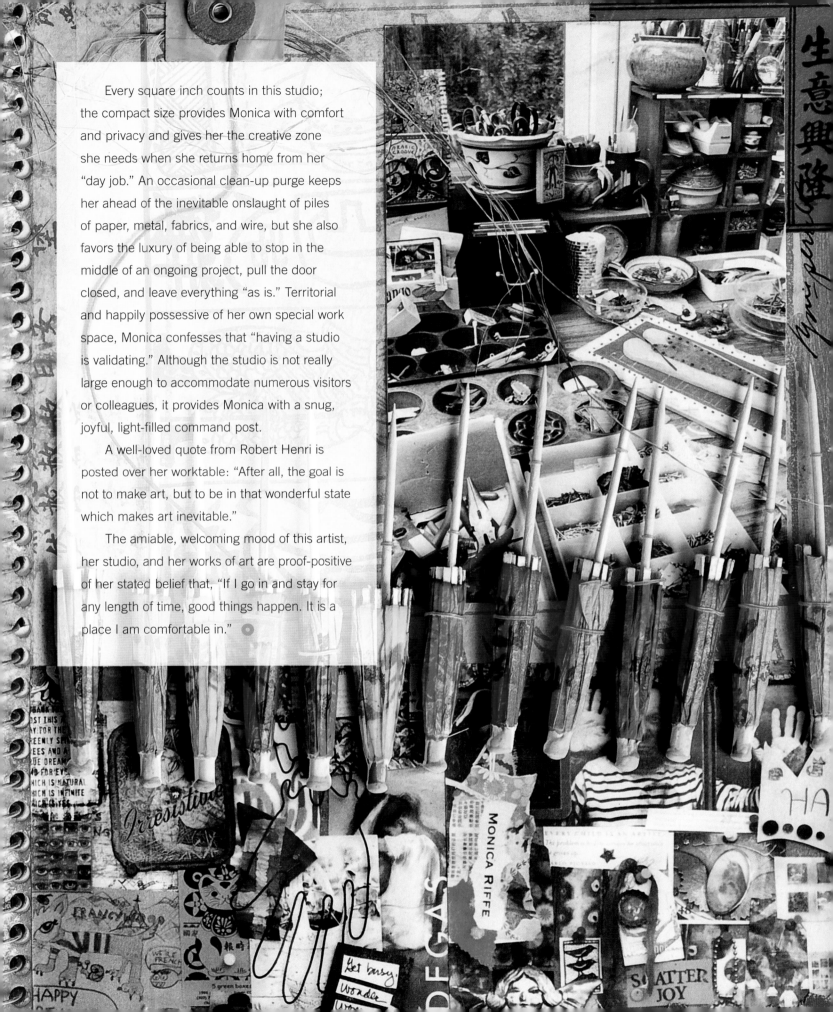

Every square inch counts in this studio; the compact size provides Monica with comfort and privacy and gives her the creative zone she needs when she returns home from her "day job." An occasional clean-up purge keeps her ahead of the inevitable onslaught of piles of paper, metal, fabrics, and wire, but she also favors the luxury of being able to stop in the middle of an ongoing project, pull the door closed, and leave everything "as is." Territorial and happily possessive of her own special work space, Monica confesses that "having a studio is validating." Although the studio is not really large enough to accommodate numerous visitors or colleagues, it provides Monica with a snug, joyful, light-filled command post.

A well-loved quote from Robert Henri is posted over her worktable: "After all, the goal is not to make art, but to be in that wonderful state which makes art inevitable."

The amiable, welcoming mood of this artist, her studio, and her works of art are proof-positive of her stated belief that, "If I go in and stay for any length of time, good things happen. It is a place I am comfortable in."

ARTIST Judi Riesch

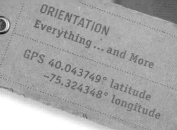

ORIENTATION
Everything ... and More
GPS 40.043749° latitude
−75.324348° longitude

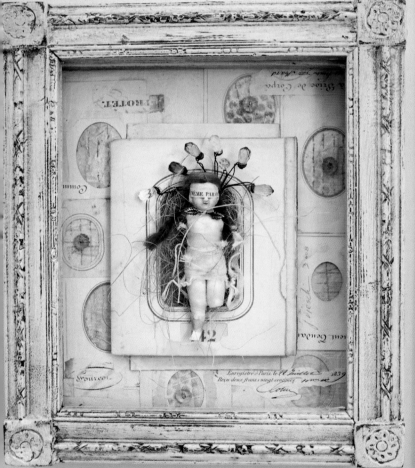

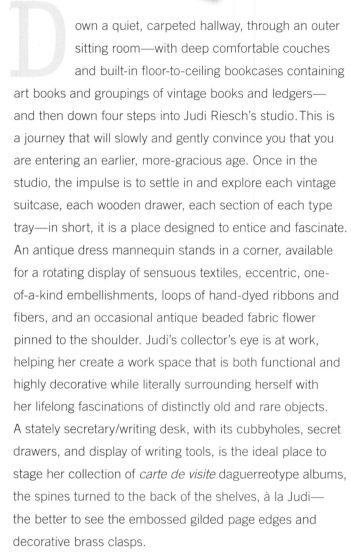

Down a quiet, carpeted hallway, through an outer sitting room—with deep comfortable couches and built-in floor-to-ceiling bookcases containing art books and groupings of vintage books and ledgers—and then down four steps into Judi Riesch's studio. This is a journey that will slowly and gently convince you that you are entering an earlier, more-gracious age. Once in the studio, the impulse is to settle in and explore each vintage suitcase, each wooden drawer, each section of each type tray—in short, it is a place designed to entice and fascinate. An antique dress mannequin stands in a corner, available for a rotating display of sensuous textiles, eccentric, one-of-a-kind embellishments, loops of hand-dyed ribbons and fibers, and an occasional antique beaded fabric flower pinned to the shoulder. Judi's collector's eye is at work, helping her create a work space that is both functional and highly decorative while literally surrounding herself with her lifelong fascinations of distinctly old and rare objects. A stately secretary/writing desk, with its cubbyholes, secret drawers, and display of writing tools, is the ideal place to stage her collection of *carte de visite* daguerreotype albums, the spines turned to the back of the shelves, à la Judi— the better to see the embossed gilded page edges and decorative brass clasps.

Clearly, her own artwork expresses a direct affinity with her surroundings and her countless collections. The hushed colors of this shadowbox, incorporating a small treasured bisque doll, old glass tack pins, and faceted etched beads, tintype frames, and her own handmade paper, reflect the mood of the studio; humble elements of wire and twine add an unexpected touch. All appear in an enclosure, a recurring theme in Judi's studio, where suitcases, small chests, French lunch carriers, cabinets, and carved boxes provide storage and endless eye candy.

JUDI RIESCH ▶

A row of four matching suitcases stand open, providing ever-changing displays of materials and collage fodder, as well as found objects. The largest case presents an array of old photos—formal studio portraits, snapshots, individuals, groups, children; the smallest contains a group of objects made of horn and tortoise shell.

A ransom of carte de visite albums, in all stages of disrepair or intentional "altering," are gathered in another suitcase, awaiting assignments. Stalwart wooden clipboards, daguerreotype cases, leather notebooks and autograph books, photo albums and girls' college scrapbooks (a specialty of Judi's) full of memorabilia fill the mostly vintage storage units. Smaller groups of objects "travel" through the studio, as Judi auditions various combinations for her assemblages, setting everything out in an uncluttered area to be considered, changed, tweaked, and finalized. Judi prizes her ability to plan and arrange multiple projects at the same time without the "need to clean up," as well as the freedom to close the door for privacy or open it wide for visitors. She also takes pleasure in using her studio space for gift-making, wrapping, and seasonal preparations. But the latest addition to the studio, a small desk and bench for her young granddaughter, brings the biggest smile.

"Aesthetics are as important to me as organization," says Judi, who likes to peruse her shelves of antique ribbons, displayed according to color, and arrange her wooden doll mannequins in a row by height. The act of arranging or staging favorite collections is often her preferred way of ramping up for a new project and engaging in research and planning phases. Sometimes, even an unconscious display of random small treasures in a nearby wooden type drawer can take on a kindred feeling to the "rare wares" that appear elsewhere in the studio and throughout her home.

Judi's love affair with elegant calligraphy, scribbled marginalia, steel-etched typography and fine penmanship has also fostered a full-out mania for antique ledger books.

JUDI RIESCH

The bountiful array of these books, normally maintained for record-keeping, listing, and notating, forms one of Judi's most favored collections. The spines line up on shelves throughout her home and her studio and present themselves in varying condition, from fragile to mint. Some of the smaller record-keeping books in her collection once functioned as daily diaries and handwritten almanacs, providing glimpses into past lives … and spurring new ideas. The serendipitous discovery of a "blotter page" tucked into an old book adds to the pleasure of the hunt and presents a reminder of a time when dip pens, ink wells, and fine handwriting were *de rigueur*.

But even a bountiful collection has to have a star. Judi's largest ledger book, and the confessed "most special" one, appears, large and in charge. This baronial volume (16" × 21" × 5" [40.6 × 53.3 × 12.7 cm]) was a serendipitous find and includes entries from 1880 to 1883, written in French. Originally part of a twenty-volume set detailing the activities of a French architectural firm, the heavy-enough-to-be-a-doorstop book is covered in softly faded green suede, with impressive brass trim on all corners and red leather touches on the cover and spine. As one carefully opens the book and begins exploring the entries, the strong appeal of the distant past is undeniable—and nothing could make Judi happier.

"And *yes*, I do use the actual pages from the ledgers—never copies. It just feels more authentic. Copies never have the depth and patina that the actual paper has."

—JUDI RIESCH

ARTIST Michelle Ward

ORIENTATION How Cool is That?
GPS 40.537005° latitude, −74.492887° longitude

Neither snow, nor rain, nor heat, nor gloom of night can deter this enthusiastic convert to the wonderful world of spray painting. And on fair, sunny days, she's likely to pull an all-day spray fest, just to take advantage of the favorable conditions, tossing the artwork down on the grass to dry. Everything Michelle Ward could possibly need to create her inventive, highly graphic artwork—spray cans, innumerable stencils, project files, clipboards, and more—is kept in rugged plastic carriers at the back door, ready to be grabbed at a moment's notice. Her spray station is located a few steps from her home and indoor studio, and all Michelle has to do is set up her worktable and position her cardboard "spray booth."

Spray painting, although a fairly recent passion, is a natural for this mixed-media artist, who prizes strong graphics, spontaneity, and a "follow your bliss" approach to everything she does. Plus, it has another undeniable component—it's just plain fun.

"I LIKE TO WORK RANDOMLY AND FAST, NOT CARING IF THE STENCIL IS PERFECTLY SPRAYED."

—Michelle Ward

Setting up her spray studio in the backyard allows Michelle quick and easy access to a suitable work area, while being within earshot of her three exuberant teenagers. Her ingenious, self-designed spray booth, made from two large cardboard cartons, provides cover for her work during windy conditions and helps contain the paint and fumes.

Even an art form as spontaneous as spray painting requires organization, and Michelle has devised a system for storing her stencils in plastic page protectors, inside three-ring binders. The binders, plus any full-sheet stencils, are kept in rugged plastic carrying bins; her supersized stencils are attached to an easel with bulldog clips.

Michelle's clever, practical solutions for arranging and storing art supplies extend to her indoor studio, which she admits is brimming with "stuff." Although visitors have been known to peek in and be overwhelmed by the visual banquet, Michelle insists that she knows where everything is. Painted wooden dressers from childhood that followed her through several moves and once provided storage in the children's rooms are now in her studio, providing memories along with drawer space. Printer trays and wall-mounted shadowboxes are used for storing tiny things and embellishments, and a former pantyhose display unit from her local pharmacy was repurposed to house row upon row of rubber stamps. A collection of Pierrot

dolls gazes down from a shelf, and a growing group of enigmatic, white Styrofoam wig heads stare straight ahead.

Winston, her black cat, has taken up permanent residence. Michelle's teens and their friends are always welcome to drop into her self-described "big playroom," and, not surprisingly, she engages them in some creative sparring.

This artist, known for gathering unexpected tiny bits and wisps of flotsam and jetsam and preserving them in journals as "evidence," has created two ultra-personal studios, one indoors and one out. Her joy—in her work and in her family—is plainly, undeniably, happily, and indisputably … evident. ◉

"I LOVE BEING IN MY STUDIO. MY COMPUTER IS SET UP IN MY STUDIO, AND ALL MY FAVORITE THINGS ARE THERE—MY CDS, MY BOOKS, MY JOURNALS, MY SUPPLIES. I AM IN THERE FOR THE BEST PART OF EVERY DAY, EVEN IF I'M NOT DOING ANY WORK."

—Michelle Ward

ORIENTATION Imagination
at Play... Page by Page
GPS 41.562130° latitude
−87.494212° longitude

LIBRARY

Many artist's lives have "second acts," in which the artist expresses a latent persistent fascination and can actually turn it into a new career. Pam Sussman's many talents served her well as a graphic designer, and these gifts have also come in handy for her present mania: one-of-a-kind artist books and limited-edition handmade journals of paper and fabric. A consummate workshop instructor, who can teach anyone to create even the most ambitious book or binding, this experienced artist and designer recalls her first "art studio"—a rolling cart with four drawers filled with rubber stamps, cardstock, a bone folder, and a handful of glitter pens. Yes, glitter pens.

Nowadays, she welcomes friends, neighbors, work shop participants, and colleagues into the latest incarnation of her studio: a large, vibrant, welcoming, well-organized finished basement that is approximately 1,800 square feet (548.6 m²), with an additional 300 square feet (91.4 m²) of unfinished space for woodworking and extra storage. The space includes a social area with a fireplace and seating, a research library, a refreshment area, the main workroom, and a full bath. Best of all, every square inch of the space is defined by Pam's unfailing eye for lively color, strong visual composition, and sensible organization.

"It is instantly apparent, as soon as you enter, that this studio is all about the books, from the display cases to the bulging library shelves."

—PAM SUSSMAN

PAM SUSSMAN ➤

With the studio's endless space for learning, constructing, and exploring unique book forms, it's little wonder that students come from all over to work with Pam during her Book Intensives. A favorite plaque that reads "Life is good!" seems to amply describe the studio environment and everything that happens here.

"My space must function efficiently. When I sit down to work, I don't want to be looking for tools and supplies—I want to get started right away! Items are stored close to where they are used. Contents of closed storage boxes are labeled, not only to help me remember what is inside but also to help students find their own way when I am not available. Every tool that I need to make a book is reachable from my spin chair.

"Beyond that, I want to feel happy and excited to be in the space. There is always something interesting to look at, something new and untried left out to explore—a new book or magazine, new art supplies, a model of something that has captured my interest, luscious papers brought by a friend."

PAM SUSSMAN ▶

"Books meet each new encounter without any need for their batteries to be recharged, software upgraded, or chips replaced. But it is the densely informative immediacy and intimacy of the experience provided by books which is at the heart of their longevity."

—JOHANNA DRUCKER,
The Century of Artists' Books

Form follows function in Pam's studio. A large cutting table for paper and boards is equipped with the appropriate tools and surrounded by organized bins and drawers. A sewing table adjoins the storage bins for fabric and drawers filled with thread and fiber embellishments. Pam's work-station consists of a large kitchen table and a swivel work chair. From this command post, she can spin around to retrieve tools, a book press, a sewing frame, or other supplies, all within arm's reach. Additional white tables fill the main workroom, providing work space for visiting students, drying surfaces for paste papers, and holding areas for various book components, including kits and editions; it's a seemingly endless space for any need that might arise in the studio.

Approximately 125 labeled drawers and over 70 open wire drawers hold "the stuff:" materials, tools, markers, pencils, pens, rubber bands, stamps, linen, wire, and more.

Carts are also a favorite storage solution in Pam's studio because they can easily be wheeled to worktables and whisked back to the storage area when Pam is finished. A sturdy red cart from a local hardware store holds two dozen bricks, covered in book cloth, used to weight glued surfaces while they dry. Other carts contain paper punches and binding machines.

An impressive array of Pam's handmade artist books, of almost every description, size, configuration, and format, are presented on a handsome angular display unit. The shape of the display unit seems perfectly in sync with the various measuring tools, dividers, compasses, T-squares, and triangles necessary to create masterful one-of-a-kind books.

She's thought of everything.

PAM SUSSMAN ▶

"Books have the most powerful and subtle connotations. They are never only objects, they have a voice with which they speak across time and across lives, a voice contingent only in part on their material nature and expressed forcefully in their text."

—**PHILIPP BLOM,**
To Have and To Hold

With a studio overflowing with aesthetically pleasing and practical storage solutions, it is surprising to hear Pam confess to having a favorite. However, she admits to having a special fondness for her ten-drawer flat file. Possibly, her true affection is for the drawer after drawer filled with the most luscious papers she has found on her travels or have been given to her by colleagues and students. Coming in handy are repurposed storage items, including several antique wooden divided trays and CD storage units outfitted with small baskets for tiny fabric embellishments or very small books. A wall-hung storage unit for rubber stamps made by Pam's husband has had a prominent place in all Pam's studios, and it continues to provide space for stamps that are current favorites.

Music, in the form of her favorite local radio station or from an endless supply of CDs, is a constant companion in the studio, even during workshops, when jazz, sound-scapes, New Age, Celtic, or rock music fills the studio and urges everyone on.

"Virtually all my creative activities happen in the studio," says the proprietor of this welcoming, super-efficient work-space. "Grounded. Happy. Stimulated." These are the words that Pam uses to describe how she feels in this special, distinctive environment. "There will never be enough time to explore it all," she says. But, at least, when she is ready to work, everything will be right at her fingertips. ○

ARTISTS Linda & Opie O'Brien

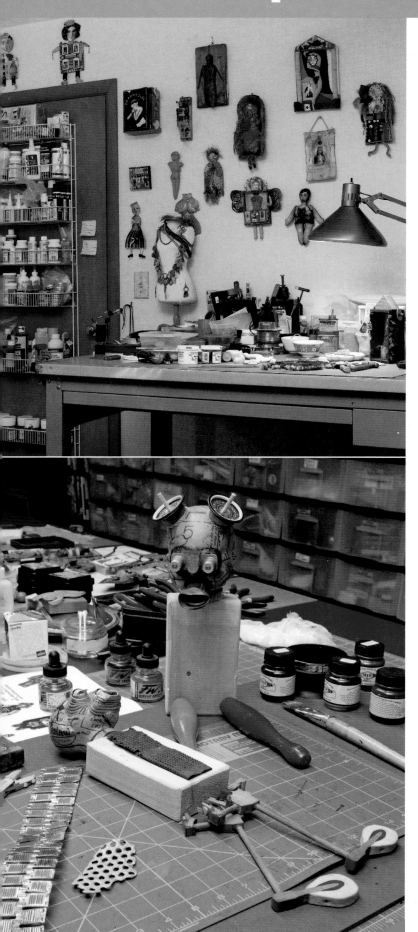

ORIENTATION
Four Hands Clapping
GPS 41.813213° latitude
-81.199619° longitude

In a telling revelation, Opie describes in detail the O'Brien's overflowing, cascading, repurposed work environments for creating art and producing music … and then adds, "I cannot exclude a pertinent aspect of my studio—its proximity to Lake Erie." He describes his connection to nature, the scenic sunsets, the long walks and serendipitous discoveries as "pure joy." One can imagine the O'Briens carrying their shoreline finds back to the house, Opie heading for his jewelry bench and Linda finding a place to work inside the screened-in porch.

When the O'Briens decided to teach mixed-media art workshops full time, the decision precipitated major changes in their living and working environments—all of which seem to have produced ideal long-term solutions. Each maintains a separate working environment as well as a shared space in which they enjoy collaborating on everything from new workshop ideas to writing books and articles. Even when in their own inner sanctums, they are still likely to call out to one another on a regular basis: "Hey … do you have a minute?" A large workroom contains countless tools, a kiln area, a copy and printer center with four copy machines, custom storage for specialty papers, work sinks, an acetylene torch with an exhaust-fan setup, approximately 350 clear plastic drawers for storing "visual offerings," and much more.

After years of uprooting their extensive studio tools and materials for teaching engagements on the road, they have perfected an efficient travel setup to reduce the inevitable disarray and confusion following workshops. Sensible solutions, arrived after living and working in the space over time, make the whole environment personal, organic, and practical.

LINDA & OPIE O'BRIEN ▶

Because their interests occasionally diverge, Linda has a private studio devoted to jewelry making and art dolls that includes a sewing station; Opie has a sound-proof music studio that occasionally doubles as a photography darkroom. Their special treasures happen all throughout the space: Linda's collection of art dolls (her own work and figures made by colleagues) is displayed above her worktable; Opie's vintage tin space toys, rocket ships, and robots share the studio with a collection of masks gathered in Mexico.

Opie describes his unique method for capturing unanticipated ideas for future projects: If an unrelated-but-inspiring object is found during a search of the studio, he places the item on a yellow tray as a "reminder" of the impulse, rather than having a good idea slip away. "I have dozens of these trays that I know are potential future projects," he says.

He likens his studio, which provides a nurturing enveloping environment, to a cocoon, explaining that he can literally reach up and touch the seven-foot (2 m) ceilings above his head. He prefers cross-pollinating mediums and techniques, often combining disparate elements and using the different studio areas to achieve varying effects. Depending on the project and its demands, a piece can be worked on using torches, wood-burning tools, encaustic wax, and more in the various areas, before eventually ending up in a clean area, where finishing takes place.

Linda describes herself as dualistic by nature and enjoys the luxury of having an office in which she can take care of computer tasks and business correspondence as well as a jewelry bench, at which she can follow her muse and lose all track of time. Both artists consider their space, created as a mutual collaboration, as a sanctuary—a place where each of them can pursue ideas and bounce ideas off each other and brainstorm and laugh a lot. ◉

Ellen Kochansky's commitment to using and reusing fabrics is symbolized by the so-called bricks that she creates, using past generations of fabrics from her quilt stash and recycled garments that find their way to her studio. A charismatic vintage industrial cloth saw, "The Wolf," is used to cut through innumerable layers of fabrics, and these are stacked, wrapped, and dipped in beeswax to form the innovative bricks that compose a faux hearth in her studio. The heavy-duty saw, first purchased as mere sculpture, was eventually restored and revived by a friend, and it soon became a reliable, useful piece of equipment in her studio environment. It shares space with row upon row of brown cardboard storage files, bales of natural plant material, and shelves full of neutral-hued fabrics, canvas, handmade papers, and almost anything else that reminds Ellen of her passion for naturals. This artist, who finds uncommon beauty in the most common things, once papered the walls of a studio with brown Kraft paper and never passes up the chance to buy another wheel-sized spool of metal dressmaker pins, simply because they appeal to her confident aesthetic.

"...AS WE SORT AND RE-SORT AND PONDER HOW TO ALLOW OURSELVES JUST ONE MORE ACQUISITION, WE RUN OUR MATERIALS THROUGH OUR FINGERS, AND THEY TALK TO US."

—Ellen Kochansky

LKO

ELLEN KOCHANSKY
1237 MILE CREEK RD
PICKENS, SC 29671
P&F | 864-868-4250
EKochansky@gmail.com

An entire wall of neutral-themed fabrics, secured with sturdy binder clips and sorted according to earth/jewel/water/granite hues, underlines Ellen's great respect for the mechanics of color and the subtleties of nature and provides inventory control for an ever-burgeoning stash.

A self-described pack rat, Ellen insists the rollicking abundant nature of her studio, with materials kept out in the open where they can ignite ideas, pleases her. Known for a color palette of cool hushed tones and soothing visual textures, she approaches each new project with focused ebullience and stand-up-and-cheer enthusiasm. Her ideas for commissions and workshops are hatched here, amid bales of fabrics and her favorite art materials. "I'm blessed by this space," Ellen declares, "and I love it here."

Welcome to a private enclave, in which work, creativity, visualizations, and energy coalesce, a self-described place of discovery and fulfillment. An artist who strongly values her solitude and privacy, Maria Moya has designed and created a studio brimming with her own personal delights, from the endless patterned papers she collects to the unique and eccentric containers she brings home from travels to hold studio accoutrements.

Although the studio is rarely open to visitors, except by appointment, it almost always appears in a highly visual and arranged state—an extension of Maria's personal aesthetic, which embraces beauty in all forms. Every aspect of her home and work space is arranged with an eye for fascinating detail and composition; it is a constant kaleidoscope of color, pattern-on-pattern, texture, and personal documentation. A saved exotic candy wrapper, a wisp of coiled fiber in an unexpected color, packaging from a nearby Asian market, a museum postcard: All of these small wonders inform and inspire Maria, and every flash of inspiration is preserved in compact, ever-changing tabletop tableaux throughout the studio.

Maria confesses to having a passion for black-and-white, as well as anything with a checkerboard pattern. Throughout the studio, storage containers of every description are arranged and curated with a careful eye. Most of the unique vessels, boxes, vases, baskets, and tins are handpicked to perform some duty in the studio, while bringing a sense of beauty and harmony to the overall desk-scape. Her studio recently underwent a major redesign to respond to new technology, different tools, and a revised storage plan. With her design library, fabric stash, and cutting areas relocated to a different area in her home, Maria's main studio performs more efficiently.

MARIA C. MOYA ▶

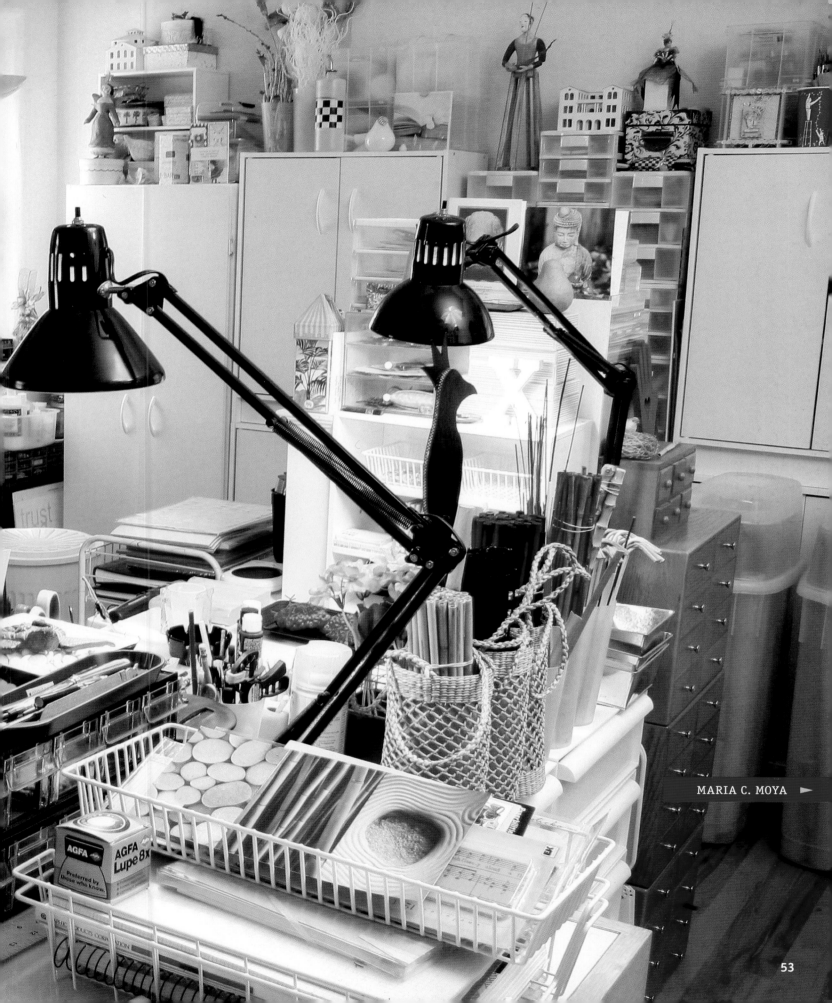

MARIA C. MOYA ▶

53

Maria's favorite storage ideas? "Recycled, clear plastic containers for organic salad greens from the health food store. Black and white baskets in every size. Boxes covered in interesting geometric papers, for both storage and eye candy. Stainless steel containers with glass lids. Porcelain toothbrush holders for brushes. A twenty-seven-drawer metal auto-supply tool cabinet. Wooden serving trays for separating various projects or for a portable workstation when needed."

Her recent work—a series of small, exquisite vessels in the form of tiny boats or gondolas—is a reflection of her gift for finding the maximum possibilities in virtually every object she encounters. Inside this quiet, mostly white room, Maria celebrates "the world of art that I live in every day." ◉

"My goal is to maximize the creative juices when they are exploding and overflowing. My space functions and keeps me organized and efficient. When working on various pieces at one time, a dance occurs in the studio that leads to another discovery, a new embellishment, the birth of a new work of art."

—MARIA MOYA

DISCOVERY
CONSISTS NOT
IN SEEKING NEW
LANDSCAPES
BUT IN HAVING
NEW EYES

(MARCEL PROUST)

ORIENTATION
The Best Tree Fort Ever
GPS 40.037774° latitude
−75.276053° longitude

Quick, grab an umbrella. A sprint across the lawn, amid a sudden summer shower, and then we are tucked inside the welcoming studio. Bee Shay calls it her nest, her art home. Actually, her two-story studio is a compact vintage barn structure behind her home, the floor-to-ceiling windows giving her a bird's-eye view of her surroundings. Outside, the rain drenches the trees (and one of the playful dogs), but inside is a private world, where every furnishing, every bibelot, every saved element of nature has personal meaning to this artist, who prizes sentimentality above all else.

After climbing the stairs to the second floor of the studio, where Bee's worktables and storage are, one enters a large room that is seemingly full of saved and salvaged wooden furnishings and architectural details. Disparate windows, rescued from other structures, are tucked and cobbled into every spare location. A large French door opens directly onto a wooded banked terrace behind the studio, and Bee cautions that a neighbor's horse often strolls by. "Just be prepared," she says with a smile.

BEE SHAY ▶

A mere 100 yards (91.4 m) from her home, where reality, Internet service, reported dust bunnies, and household chores reside, the barn communicates a strong feeling of an enchanted getaway, a place to indulge dreams and follow impulses, while surrounded by well-loved things. Upstairs is chock-a-block with worktables, bookcases, plenty of storage (mostly inside antique cabinets, chests, and suitcases), tableaux of her favorite things, and completed works of art. Downstairs is a living area with comfortable seating and a compact, welcoming kitchen featuring more salvaged doorframes, windows, and countless wooden surfaces. The lower floor is a place to put up your feet; the top level ignites ideas and welcomes "art all-nighters" when the mood strikes.

The old book press within, and the trees, lawn, and the clapboard home without. No wonder the artist describes her time in the studio as "Happy. Fulfilled. Honest."

> "The vital connection is that my studio is an extension of me … it gives me a place to get out of my head, get out of my way, and do the work."
>
> —BEE SHAY

This artist, who grew up surrounded by nature, defines herself as eclectic. She sees this enduring quality reflected in the infinite variety of the outdoors and is drawn to any natural object that is odd or unusual, smooth or barbed, feathered or fibrous. Downstairs, a large antique model of a frame house seems to suggest the barn in-progress, and the staircase leading up to the studio provides a sneak preview of the wonders to be found above. An old blackboard at the top of the stairs invites visitors to leave a message, and a tangle of canvas work aprons hang on a peg by the door, at the ready.

Having a dedicated space for making art has validated Bee's decision to become a full-time creative person, and she reveals how her studio space started out with a very specific plan and then (just like life) evolved into a wonderfully organic outcome, all its own.

Some of Bee's favorites? Antiques—things that have been held, worn, fondled, read, things that carry a richness of history and tell of previous lives; three sand dollars from a beach near Puget Sound; a glass stopper found years ago on a beach in Maryland, while walking with her mother; a grouping of feathers, presented in a container, near her writing desk; beach glass; things to hoard, things to use, things to give.

Modern plastic storage containers seem out of sync with the woodsy, tree house atmosphere here, so Bee relies on old carpenter's-tool carriers, vintage printer's type drawers, wooden boxes, mason jars, smooth wooden bowls overflowing with shells, curls of birch, dried branches, and patches of moss. An eye-high stack of old travel cases greets visitors at the top of the wooden steps, and the prevailing mood inside the studio is a hybrid of nature-study center, deep-woods Adirondack cabin, and Northwest fishing camp. Fellow artists are welcome here, the two big worktables providing pull-up-a-chair ambience and efficient work space. And then there are all those drawers full of fascinating things to explore, ideas to discuss, music to play, and two big yellow dogs to pet. It's still raining. Why not stay awhile?

ORIENTATION
Gentle Tsunami
GPS 41.964270° latitude
−73.440469° longitude

She lives and works not far from an historic covered bridge, in a church that was built in 1790. A private freight train clatters past her front door on narrow old tracks, and when she isn't doing art she is a stilt-walker and fire-eater. Meet Terri Moore. First-time visitors to her large vaulted studio area, full of easels, work lamps, sheaves of drawings, and stacks of paintings, are captivated by this utterly unusual space … and the artist-in-residence. A spiral staircase leads up to the choir loft, and the view "straight down" reveals a cozy corner furnished with a comfortable old arm chair, reading lamp, exotic bibelots, comfy quilts and throws, and an old record player spinning 78 rpm albums—Benny Goodman, if I'm

not mistaken. A cup of strong, brewed coffee in a giant mug, and we're ready to tour the studio.

Like many of the artists in this book, Terri's bulletin board provides a glimpse, a true view, into her seemingly endless fascinations and manias. Far more than just a collection of saved images, Terri's board is the most personal element in her studio. She describes it as a narrative of where she's been and where she's going, and as a pictorial reference and inspiration. The board is edited over time, with major changes marking the beginning of a new series of work, but with the inevitable keepers that seem to endure, no matter what.

TERRI MOORE ▶

Terri welcomes Maya, the calico cat, into the studio —or maybe it is vice versa. The tortoiseshell cat has been known to go down to the studio and call out if Terri has stayed away for a couple of days. But, overall, this artist prizes her solitude in the studio. She elaborates on the monogamous relationship with her work: "When I am looking for the truth in a piece or process, outside input can throw me off my path," she says. "Often, it's the uncomfortable places that lead to growth. The trick is to stay within this quiet place inside myself to find my own way."

Music is a welcome element, and Terri often notates what she has listened to on the backs of her paintings. She considers her studio a laboratory, in which she can totally immerse herself in both research and work. Terri defines her studio as "an environment where I can take off the armor one needs to be out and about in the world and be wholly myself as an artist." She favors having her work space set up, ready to go, "leaving a thousand threads of existing and potential ideas to pick up at any time."

The efficiency and readiness of Terri's space might rely on tools, supplies, and equipment, but one of her undeniable gifts is her eye for arranging. "I completely enjoy this process, almost to a fault," she laughs.

"At the end of long painting sessions, I like to sit and look—really *see* the space and remember it as a moment in time."

— TERRI MOORE

TERRI MOORE ▶

65

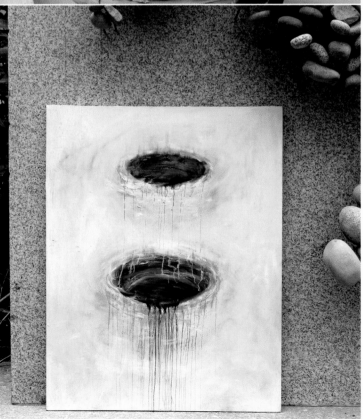

> "There is a ritual in it ...
> entering a space that is set
> up for creative work."
>
> — **TERRI MOORE**

Her studio overflows with significant, staged collections (as well as an endless wardrobe of costumes and shoes), and she considers these special belongings a weave of experiences, as well as visual compost. The time spent in her studio arranging and creating still-life compositions, which she describes as environments and visual pockets of experiences, is vital to her work.

Not surprisingly, this inveterate collector has endless alternative uses for offbeat objects. Old tool boxes, wooden and metal, hold supplies or stand open to reveal tableaux within. Vintage candleholders become pedestals for a grouping of bird's nests. Old form molds for iron railroad-engine parts —enough to fill a station wagon—that she discovered, one day, when the Collecting Gods were on her side, are enjoyed as sculptural shapes and are also used as unique containers. One of Terri's large paintings, shown here, illuminates how her collections influence her artwork and vice versa.

One Felliniesque summer evening, just at twilight, a train passed by the old church/studio, moving especially slowly. Illuminated within the vintage passenger cars were old, thrift-shop couches, drapes, and clotheslines strung with costumes. As the train slowed in front of the studio, the circus folks inside came to the window and looked out. The artist stood on her lawn, amid huge outdoor sculptures, juggling gear and fire-show props, and gardening debris. Everyone waved, and then the train picked up steam and went on its way. Was it real or imagined? In this place of intense imagination and singular fascination, *anything* can happen. And often does. ◉

ORIENTATION
Tools of the Trade
GPS 42.329675° latitude
−73.614859° longitude

Though "Renaissance Man" might be an overused title, it describes Bill Wilson perfectly. Entering his studio, I was instantly impressed with the sheer variety of art-making tools and supplies and work stations for his various interests. A large easel commands the space, with work lamps and a model stand. Sheaves of preliminary sketches are pinned to the wall nearby. All around the studio are examples of Bill's works, which include portraits and landscapes, in oils, acrylic, watercolor, and charcoal. Bill's studio commands a significant part of his one-of-a-kind home, designed by his son. His environment is a hybrid of calm Asian sensibility and deep-woods cabin, with lots of natural wood, open staircases, leather furniture, and several custom-designed niches and long continuous built-in shelves that display Bill's collections and small works of art.

Behind the house, only a couple of steps from the studio, is a compact barn that Bill uses for drilling, sawing, gluing and clamping works-in-progress. The rural shed was transformed when Bill completely laminated the exterior surface of the structure with local stone and shale found on his property. The process of resurfacing the barn was an exercise in composition, as he determined the best placement for each section of stone. Surrounded by mature trees, the small, stone-covered structure sets a handmade mood, simpatico with the mostly wooden, distinctive house. Providing an always-cool, shaded place in which to work— his indoor studio only steps away—the shed is a favorite place for Bill during the warm months.

They're all here: *Girl With a Pearl Earring,* Rouault's *The Old King,* Grant Wood's stolid *American Gothic,* and more. Bill has created a series of homage portraits, worked in oils on thin pieces of slate. This engaging lineup is the first thing one notices when entering Bill's living space, and the parade of familiar-yet-new faces keeps good company with Bill's other distinctive collections of outdoor flotsam and jetsam, books, nests, and handmade vessels. Large glass doors open onto a welcoming patio surrounded by outcroppings of stone and the quiet splash of a water feature.

BILL WILSON ▶

"The familiar objects of everyday life have become the stuff of art. In the world of art based on the found object, low becomes high and tools become art."

— **CAROLYN LARAY,** *Tools as Art*

In a corner of the studio, the numerous drawers of an old, blue flat file overflow with reference materials, papers of every description, completed drawings, studies and sketches, and more. Stacks of paintings await revision, refinement, and resurrection, and cartons of art supplies are tucked into every available corner.

Orderliness is hardly the point in this wonderfully exuberant studio that seems to declare "WORK happening here. Please wait in the garden." The studio exudes an atmosphere of joy, productivity, commitment, and vast variety. It's a place where ideas play tag, both indoors and out, and create a constant interplay of impulse and instinct.

The surrounding country landscape is revealed through each window and provides a constant presence. Fields stretch out from both sides of the house and in front and back are densely wooded areas. Several worktables within the space are overrun with a vast array of materials at the ready. Stacks of books, cartons of materials, endless art supplies, and unexpected discoveries appear throughout. Peering into a shipping carton, one is likely to discover a beautiful grouping of bird feathers or a nest of twigs found during a walk. Tiny, delicate remnants from nature—a wing, a small animal skull—are displayed randomly among small paintings (many of them self-portraits) on shelves around the perimeter of the studio. A couple of Bill's inventive work stools, the seats made from generous, rough-sawn slabs of wood, the legs from repurposed hand tools, are placed throughout the room. Work lamps are clamped here and there, and a convenient mirror is placed near the model stand.

The view, seen through one of the large windows, provides a wooded backdrop for Bill's taboret, placed next to the easel and overflowing with paints, jars, solvents, and countless brushes. For every artist who ever listed a work sink as one of their most-desired studio features,

BILL WILSON ▶

Bill's is one of the hardest-working sinks ever, reflecting the constant exploration happening in his well-used, well-loved workroom.

When does a collection become an archive? This seasoned traveler has collected endless postcards from museums and cultural outposts all over the world and gathered them in a large, wooden wine carton, separating the cards with handmade dividers to form a practical reference file and card catalog. If Bill has need of a visual reminder of, say, the Temple of Dendur, he just has to walk to the file and dig in. The file is an invaluable visual resource and a meaningful way of keeping track of ephemera that is normally easily scattered and forgotten.

Afternoon sunlight illuminates the handcrafted stone surface of the work shed, and, inside, the worktables are full of tools, clamps, measuring devices, and glues. The frankly workmanlike surfaces wear a silt of sawdust, and the smell of fresh wood shavings fills the small area, along with the mossy aroma of fresh soil. Old storage units with drawers, collected over many years, are tucked around the work area; some of them are still in use, others confirm Bill's love of distressed rusted implements.

Several examples of Bill's work appear in *Tools as Art: The Hechinger Collection*, an impressive gathering of contemporary artworks representing and incorporating tools and hardware. This quote (below) from the exhibit catalog seems to perfectly capture the unique allure of Bill's studio as well as his creative output. ⊙

"Lifting tools, these nuts and bolts of ordinary existence, out of the role of the mundane, these artists have constructed from them works of beauty and of revelation, for it is not simply tools that fascinate the artist, but the human response to them."

— **CAROLYN LARAY,**
Tools as Art

He calls his studio "The Vortex," because he often loses all sense of time and space when he is inside, "in another dimension entirely." Tracy Moore's current studio space is a strong reminder of his childhood room, which was once full of hand-built contraptions, minitools, and Rube Goldberg–esque inventions. Clearly, having a vast selection and variety of tools and specialized equipment is a recurring theme in Tracy's world, and his studio reflects that acquisitive urge. The studio, a newly constructed separate building behind his home, is accessible at a moment's notice and provides Tracy with ample room to pursue all his fascinations, from journal making to metalworking. That means plenty of space for hammering, drilling, sawing, perforating, wood-burning, cutting, piercing, and sanding.

Functionality is important, but this hands-on studio has an intensely personal look, thanks to many of Tracy's favorite belongings: ray guns, swords, masks, posters, unusual signs, and a beloved wooden stool given to him by his grandfather. Tracy loves having anything around him that will spur his imagination and keep the good vibes going—little things that amuse him. A dartboard is available for a quick game, and a gas fireplace provides a cozy, stay-a-while atmosphere. Storage solutions include newly purchased bookcases and storage cubes, as well as repurposed items such as a shoe rack used to store hammers. His desk is awash in the latest cameras and accessories to capture his imagination, and his journal bag spills open with his traveling art kit.

An advocate for "You can create anywhere," this artist, who has finally achieved Studio Nirvana, still recalls churning up endless ideas in the cramped space of his childhood bedroom. His advice for those many people who are waiting until they have the perfect, mythic, roomy, well-equipped studio before making a commitment to doing art: "Just jump in."

"THE HARDEST THING FOR ME TO DO IS FOCUS ON ONE THING. IF I'M INTO A PROJECT, I AM FINE. I LOSE TRACK OF TIME AND DON'T WANT TO QUIT. BUT, IF I HAVEN'T STARTED SOMETHING, THEN I JUST GET LOST IN THIS BLISSFUL SENSE OF PEACE THAT I GET WHEN I AM IN MY STUDIO."

–Tracy V. Moore

In Tracy's studio, there's a perfect piece of machinery for every task, including a sheer for cutting sheets of metal "like a paper cutter," a scroll saw, a mini-bandsaw, and a heavy-as-an-anvil, 100-year-old perforator, used for creating convincing editions of faux postage. Just the luxury of being able to go into the studio and commune with such a fascinating array of specialized tools and machines is enough to make this artist's mind race with ideas, and he often observes that his work space is more like a playroom.

Tracy shares the studio space with his wife, Teesha, and the design of the space is an amalgam of both of their ideas for the ideal studio. The top floor of the two-story building is divided into thirds; one His, one Hers, one a central, shared area with a large worktable for cutting and big projects. Downstairs is The Vortex, with all of

Tracy's tools and specialized equipment, plenty of power sources, and good lighting. He thinks of the space as one that is always evolving, and he enjoys the prospect that it will continue to develop and take new directions.

Tracy describes the satisfying feeling of "Ahhhh … I'm home" when he enters the studio, and he puts a lot of time into cleaning, reorganizing, and refining it. Like many artists in this book, he laments that the chaos following a large project is daunting, and cleaning up afterwards becomes part of the ritual of completing work and processing the output. When Tracy and Teesha return from giving a workshop, there are stacks of cartons to put away and sift through, a task he takes on eagerly, so that he can return to the peaceful-playful studio environment he prizes.

"BEING INSPIRED BY THE SPACE YOU ARE IN IS DEFINITELY A BONUS. MY SPACE IS ABSOLUTELY PERSONAL."

—Tracy V. Moore

ORIENTATION Home Turf, with Flying Colors
GPS 39.949656° latitude
−105.020682° longitude

Faye's workroom/studio has all of the carefully designed style and precision of her award-winning quilts. She's mastered the art of "what to leave in, what to leave out," not only in the design of her space but in every wall-hanging and hand-quilted garment. The formerly unfinished basement of her three-story townhouse has become a well-equipped, carpeted, ultra-cozy space used for sewing, calligraphy, book arts, and collage. Comfortable seating, lots of efficient table space, good lighting, plenty of well-equipped closets, and ample bookshelves contribute to a work space that makes visitors want to stay indefinitely and enjoy a display of Faye's remarkable needle skills. "Coming from a quilting background, I want my studio to have warmth and comfort, like the other rooms in my home," says Faye. Mission accomplished.

With everything readily at hand, Faye finds it easy to get focused and begin working. Music is important for boosting energy in the studio, and a computer is available for working with photos and word processing, although Faye resists the distractions of emailing and Web-surfing in the studio.

Many of her decorative furnishings and accessories, which come from a dry-goods store Faye once owned, have special meaning. Many of these sewing-related antiques and fixtures originated in Kansas; they now blend easily with her crisp, contemporary color scheme that provides the perfect backdrop for her own spectacular wall-hung quilts. The fixtures include an old spool cabinet, drawers for displaying needles, a flower-seed display case used to arrange her vast rainbow of threads, and a huge pair of brass shears that was once a sign for a European tailor's shop. Visitors are welcome, and she especially enjoys meeting with other quilters—including groups of touring Japanese quilt-makers, who stop by for an afternoon of kindred enjoyment.

"What quilts have brought to the viewing of art generally is the intervening layer of silence, of collected thought and concerted attention."

— **RADKA DONNELL,** *Quilts As Women's Art*

Keeping things lively, Faye's irrepressible toy poodle, Delphine, is a constant source of delight, both upstairs and down in the studio. She's right at home, nestled amongst Faye's museum-quality quilts on a rocking chair in an upstairs reading nook, as cozy and entitled as any pet could be.

"Containers are a weakness with me," Faye confesses. Her extensive travels usually result in finds for the studio: painted or carved ethnic boxes, coconut shells, gourds—anything with a lid. What to put inside? That decision will inevitably come. Storage is always welcome for Faye, who often wonders if she will ever have the chance to work with all the art supplies she has amassed.

Although the room is filled with fun materials, it never has the feeling of disorder or chaos. The hand and eye of the quilter keeps everything calm. Bookcases holding color-arranged fabrics and her research library line up behind Faye's sewing station. In progress is a series of quilted, appliquéd panels that document many worldwide cultures and use their traditional motifs, iconography, and patterns. In many cases, these design elements originated before written history and are now being reprised through Faye's hand-stitched, vibrant work. ◉

Although it isn't unusual for an artist to remark that his work space reflects his interests and fascinations, Keith's studio actually bears a resemblance to his well-known, coveted mixed-media works of art and found-object jewelry. A visiting colleague once commented that stepping into Keith LoBue's studio was a bit like inhabiting one of his works of art, a revelation that inspired both visitor and artist.

This compact and efficient studio, just two steps down from Keith's living space, suits him perfectly. After moving into his home, Keith set about designing his work space, keeping in mind ergonomics and maximizing the small footprint of the room, while creating a welcoming environment. He observes that, while a spacious studio would certainly provide better storage and more free space, his snug, cave-like environment seems to contain him perfectly —"like hand in glove." Pressed for a word to define his work space, Keith offers "sanctuary" and says that he always enters the room with a sense of anticipation, eager to launch into new creative territory.

He describes feeling fully supported by his surroundings, which are designed with functionality and ensure that an array of his specialized tools are always at hand. "For me, the tools themselves feature prominently in the work space," Keith says. "Although I have some of them stored in boxes, most are hung in front of my bench at the ready. As I work, I like to be able to glance up and see the tool I need. Somehow, seeing the tools there waiting unlocks the possibilities in my mind and puts me in that crucial intuitive mode of making. Above all else, my studio has to facilitate a functional work flow for me, and so I try to eliminate unnecessary things."

LIGHT IN FRONT OF STATION NAME
INDICATES TRAIN STOPS AT THAT STATION

KEITH LOBUE ▶

Among the necessities is an unending host of found objects and small, offbeat metal and wooden discoveries, all requiring some form of organization. Old, 16 mm film canisters discovered at a local recycling shop became an ideal storage solution, and the labeled canisters stack easily on the shelves of the studio. In yet another example of reclaiming and repurposing, Keith showed up with a flatbed truck at the geology department of the local university to rescue two massive wooden cabinets, which now provide handsome studio storage.

Every new and old material offers a new challenge, so Keith's studio is set up to be flexible and functional; his soldering table, for example, converts to a lampworking station within minutes. With the exception of music in the studio, which he considers essential, all distractions have been eliminated, and this sacred space is reserved strictly for jewelry and object making. "When a particular piece of music is on, it is reflected in the choices I make, in terms of materials and techniques," Keith says. "It brings me farther into that hermetic world, free from outside distractions."

His ability to find everything efficiently at arm's length was tested one night during the inky darkness of a power outage, the ultimate test of an artist's familiarity with his space … and his willingness to keep working, no matter what!

Keith describes his studio as "intensely private—a joyful environment that encourages what I love best." Asked whether having a "real" studio makes a difference, he reveals that it is a basic necessity to have a dedicated work space for his tools and his chosen palette, found objects. But, most importantly, he feels that a studio (a habitat for making art) represents the permission every artist gives himself to engage in creativity. ◉

KEITH LOBUE ▶

FINDINGS

CHORS   NAILS   SCREWS   ABRASIVES   SHARPIES

his inner life, by Keith LoBue

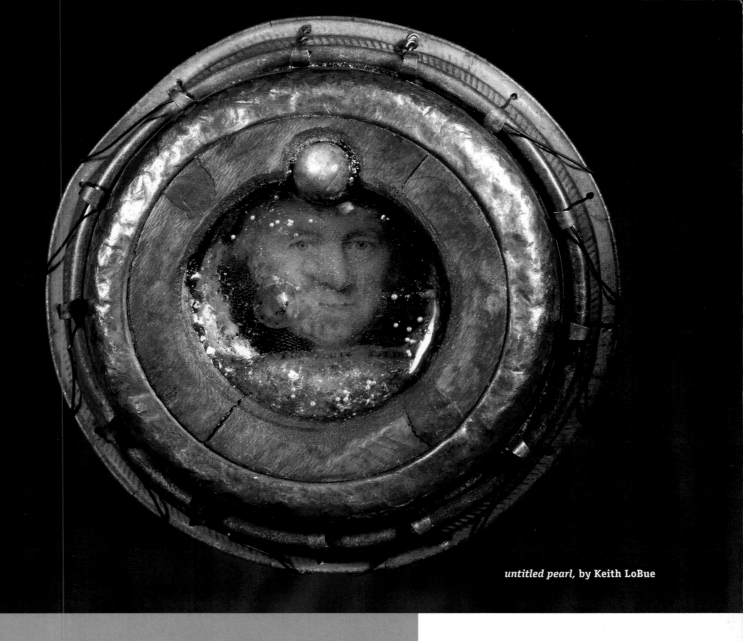

untitled pearl, by Keith LoBue

"Because of my love for all things old and timeworn, as the years have passed, I've slowly acquired antique tools to make my work. It's my ultimate vision to have all of my tools be of similar vintage. Until that time, there will be a combination of old and new rubbing elbows all around me as I work."

— KEITH LOBUE

ORIENTATION
Home Coming

GPS 37.858665° latitude
-122.261597° longitude

When does the novelty of having a brand-new studio wear off? Probably never.

Only a few short steps from Sas Colby's house, this dedicated space just for art making, with access to her gardens and outdoor seating, is a revelation. Sas carefully planned every aspect of her new work space from the ground up, and, although the 200-square-foot (61 m²) structure is considerably smaller than her previous warehouse studio spaces, she says that it is "totally my place."

The new space came along at a time in Sas' life when she was ready for something completely uncluttered and minimal. The necessity to pare down, sort through, edit, toss, and reorganize was a welcome challenge. Out with the old bulky rolling carts for paints, and in with sleek storage units and worktables on casters. The upstairs storage loft is accessible by a rolling library ladder, an apt choice for this seminal figure in book arts.

"I love having a view of my garden from the studio," says Sas. The soaring windows connect her to the outdoors and literally create a glass house, with windows on two sides and plenty of light (one of her requirements). In warm weather, the doors open, and access to the outdoors expands the work space even farther. Other must-haves: a sink, a large painting wall, a floor surface that is okay for messes, wall space to use as a pin board, music, and a doggie bed for Boris, of course.

Other than her art work, what makes the space "all Sas"? A grouping of small talismans from many travels. Two Buddha figures from Asia, a Day of the Dead skeleton from Mexico, some dried roses. A familiar holdover from three previous studios—a vintage postcard of the Mona Lisa—smiles at Sas from the corner, completely at home.

A space solely dedicated to creating artwork became a vital necessity to Sas, after she experienced having her first real studio in Taos, New Mexico, in 1991. After that, there was no turning back. Her studio is the place where she shows up to work, an inner sanctum, as well as a private place to explore. Once she's there, ideas flow, and the studio becomes a place of action.

Sas compares her many experiences with inhabiting generic studios in artists' colonies during residencies to her personal, newly constructed studio. In both cases, she says, it is about initiating the space, about claiming it and making it one's own. A canvas goes up on the wall, the paints come out, the work begins. In the earliest days in her new studio, Sas marveled at the novelty of having a studio only a couple of steps from her home. But there were some adjustments. Because of the space requirements, she needed to find a new rhythm of working on only one project at a time. The disruption of her life during the year and a half of construction required yet another adjustment. Like any new and important venture, the move into the new studio brought gradually unfolding new awarenesses and rewards.

Spring is right around the corner. The new plantings will be going in soon. The doors of the studio will be open, and a fresh canvas will go up on the wall. Everything begins anew. ○

"Having a studio encourages concentration and allows me to go deeper into my thoughts and art process. My studio *demands* expressiveness."
— **SAS COLBY**

ORIENTATION
Vision Quest

GPS 42.055696° latitude
−73.652912° longitude

This spacious, well-lit, professional printmaking studio is the outcome of many refinements, adjustments, additions, and contemplations. Perhaps the path to the perfect studio began when Steve Sorman was a nineteen-year-old college student at the University of Minnesota, renting a cheap, derelict commercial space. Ten studios and many years later, his current space is a 1,200-square-foot (365.8 m²) tractor and equipment garage, converted to suit his needs and created mostly with his own hands. Most people would consider it a coup just to have Steve's abilities as a printmaker, but this proficient artist is also a woodworker and an accomplished cook. As a result, he has constructed most of the flat files, worktables, and storage units in the studio to his specific requirements.

Steve arranges his brushes and frequently used tools within arm's reach, "much the same as you would arrange a kitchen." The studio is a reflection of his many abilities and interests—no wonder it radiates with personal energy and confidence.

"The occasional visitor is most welcome. That person or persons surely knows something I don't, and finding out makes my task all the more pleasant."

— **STEVE SORMAN**

STEVE SORMAN

This exhibition is dedicated to the memory of my friend, Shelly Ross

93

Once inside his studio, Sorman is surrounded by his tools, materials, favorite reference books, and his own artwork. Completed work is stored in large sliding drawers, and works-in-progress are tacked up on the studio walls. As he works on a new suite of prints, the generous, well-equipped work space is an ideal laboratory for exploration. The stalwart, black etching press commands a vital segment of the studio, and several glass countertops for mixing inks are located throughout the space. Open shelving is stacked with paints, dyes, inks, and solvents, all within easy reach. A host of brayers in every size, most of them made by Steve, are available for inking relief prints.

To even the most casual onlooker, the array of tools and equipment presents a mood of organization, thorough knowledge, and expertise. For others, familiar with Steve's fluid and distinctive line quality and sensuous color palette, a visit to the studio is a rare chance to observe a master printmaker at work.

"The phrase I've uttered more than any other over the past forty years is, 'I'm going to the studio.'"

— **STEVE SORMAN**

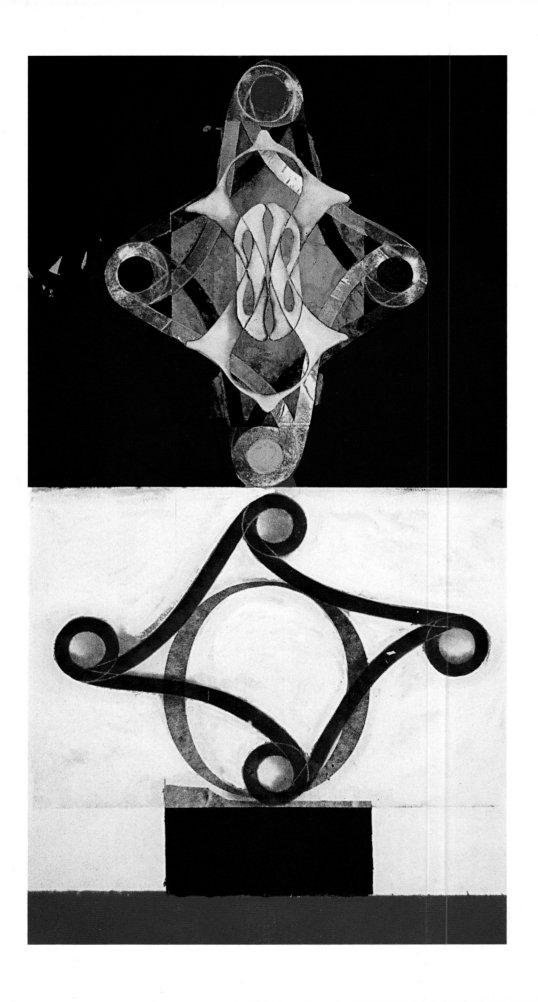

outside world, by Steven Sorman
48.5" × 26" (123.2 × 66 cm)
rust, copper oxide, sumi, acrylic,
collage on TGL handmade and
Nepalese papers

Even the most functional objects in the studio—large spackle buckets, a canopy of cheesecloth rags for scrubbing down printing plates, a coiled watering hose used in the adjacent greenhouse—add to the overall workmanlike atmosphere. The frank functionality of these elements, appearing in the midst of countless completed intaglio prints, preliminary proofs, and sheaves of exotic handmade papers, provides a glimpse into the life of an artist who goes to the studio every day. The morning might begin with lawn mowing or weed-whacking, but inevitably the path leads to the studio, where Steve describes himself as imminently at home. "I have spent more of my life in the studio than any other place on the planet," he says. "It's the perfect place for me to be."

A large caramel-colored leather chair provides seating (mostly for the cat) as Steve moves through the space, getting ready for another day … in the studio, of course. ◉

> "I've always found that it takes time to get used to a new studio, but once you do, it's like being 'in your skin'."
>
> — **STEVE SORMAN**

STEVE SORMAN ▶

"Rosa Bonheur picked up one of her palettes—Emerald green, Veronese green, cobalt green, chrome-oxide green, cobalt blue, ultramarine, Prussian blue, silver white, Naples yellow, yellow ocher, gold ocher, burnt gold ocher, raw and burnt sienna, vermillion Number One, Venetian red, Indian red, Van Dyck red, red ocher, burnt lake, madder lake, Van Dyck brown, ivory black, peach black."

— **ANNA KLUMPKE,** *Flammarion*

I n a quiet corridor, just outside the studio, a handsome Iranian apothecary cabinet stands guard.

My curiosity is getting the best of me. I asked Melissa Zink about the contents of all those mysterious drawers. Although "too numerous to mention" would have been a perfectly reasonable response, Melissa was kind enough to enumerate some of her special treasures and talismans: a polished gourd container from Japan, an old drill-bit organizer with a Taureg wedding ring on the top, lacquered painted boxes with brass clasps from India, an African necklace made from two boar's teeth, a mold from a significant small sculpture, a silver frame studded with *milagros,* a two-part container made of smooth burnished teak—and that's just the beginning. Without ever seeing the contents, I enjoyed imagining so many colors, textures, histories, ethnicities, patterns, and surfaces tucked into the multiple drawers.

Once inside the studio, one becomes aware of Melissa's eager fascination and curiosity about old things, specifically books, typography, vestments and textiles, alphabets, and architectural fragments, to name only a few. "Why is 'old' so appealing now, and when did that appeal begin?" she asks, wondering aloud. I've often wondered about that myself, and I discovered some answers in her studio. A recent series of work came about when she impulsively acquired an unreasonable number of wooden type drawers. Filling the various compartments, working with the overview of light/dark and creating the perfect something for each segment, became an ongoing project, and, eventually, several of the trays were completed. As one who never tires of books in any form, Melissa decided to hinge each tray and create an upright, standing book—the impulse was "pure Zink." The day I visited her studio, two of the books stood open on a sunny windowsill, near a row of African violets. The upright volumes reminded me of ancient choir books I once saw in Siena, Italy.

"The twelve north-facing windows, now tree-shaded, frame Taos Mountain."

— **MELISSA ZINK**

MELISSA ZINK ▶

101

The interplay of New versus Old is a significant aspect of Melissa's studio. For example, she has translated a huge visual archive of old typography, text, titles, and quotations into polymer stamps that she uses in her mixed-media assemblages. The contemporary red metal tool chest above her desk holds drawer after drawer of unmounted polymer dies, most of them stained from enthusiastic use. A row of molds for her distinctive bronze figural sculptures look down on the work surface, and the nearby bulletin board is replete with photos of dogs and cats. Melissa confesses that most visitors are disappointed with the prosaic appearance of the studio; obviously, they haven't explored the countless sliding drawers and cabinets full of vintage book fragments, prized ephemera, marbled endpapers from old volumes, book plates, and manuscripts. Little wonder that one of her large mixed-media works was titled *From the Archives of a Book Person*. Quite so.

Her studio is composed of three rooms, one for storage and making stamps; one a rough studio with band saw, grinders, lathe, and mold-making supplies; and one the expansive, windowed room shown here. Being in this studio almost every day for twelve years, Melissa says: "I like my studio. It functions well."

Book lovers need a place to commune with their volumes, a place in which to curl up and read or place sticky notes into visual reference books, to pull down a book that was thought to be lost ("Oh, *here* you are …") or take the wrapping off a new volume and begin without delay. This welcoming, cozy study, adjacent to Melissa's studio, holds her favorite volumes, personal bibelots, and a fortuitous collection of old books (some from the sixteenth century) that she found in a secondhand shop.

TOUS DROITS DE REPRODUCTION
ET DE TRADUCTION RÉSERVÉS
POUR TOUS LES PAYS, COPYRIGHT
BY *REVUE DES JEUNES* 1923

MELISSA ZINK ▶

103

"I think I can say now that the center I have been circling around and around is a private aesthetic formed from books and by books."

—MELISSA ZINK

ARTIST Armando López

Driving down a narrow, packed-dirt road, one sees a magnificent mountain ahead and hears the reassuring sounds of a nearby stream. Endless varieties of tall grasses and reeds frame the pathway to the studio, forming a serene, protective nest for this private enclave. Just inside the front doorway of the house, Armando López' self-described corner spills over with his art materials and a bounty of his well-known, mixed-media sculptural figures and oil paintings. The studio, a mere 15 square feet (4.6 m²) of space, just a step away from a sun-filled kitchen, is bursting with easels, cartons, bags of supplies, works in progress, and exuberant bales of natural materials at the ready. Armando's swivel chair puts him within reach of anything he might need, and he confesses that his studio "just developed where there was space."

He occasionally speculates that a different studio, apart from his living area, might be a better solution, but clearly the present arrangement provides inspiration, coziness, and immediate availability to his organic gardens, outdoor seating areas, and the fields of abundant grasses that play an important role in his artwork. Born in Mexico, and heavily influenced by the richly cultural traditions of his ancestors, Armando's early fascination with handcrafted altar figures and colonial santos led him to create his own versions from both traditional and contemporary materials. A chorus of his expressive and wonderfully crafted angels and deities dangle on delicate wires from the hand-hewn beams of the workroom and attest to the artist's love of disparate materials, both humble and rare.

Armando's swivel chair puts him within reach of anything he might need, and he confesses that his studio "just developed where there was space."

ARMANDO LÓPEZ ▶

"My studio is an extension of my artist's mind. I spend so much time there it is like a cocoon."

— **ARMANDO LÓPEZ**

An artist who spends most of his waking hours creating, Armando prefers to think of his studio space as a hard-working and functional area, where supplies are stacked on shelves and on the floor. He readily admits to a no-frills, comfortable approach to arranging his work space, and he defines the uninterrupted hours at his easel as "consuming and nourishing." Sometimes he listens to music in the studio, but he mostly depends on his own inner dialogue and engagement with ideas to guide his work. He values having a working space that is solely dedicated to the art-making process, a place that is always ready and brimming with his preferred materials.

The open door lets in warm summer breezes, enticing aromas from the herb garden, and a curious friend. The sun-filled corridor leading to the rest of the house extends a verdant invitation to come inside.

Chaos and order rule in this ultra-personal and inviting space, depending on the artist's mood and the ingenuity of his hands, but one constant is the strong focus and dedication that he brings to his exquisite handcrafted figural sculptures. With wings, crowns, diadems, exotic headpieces, and multicultural trappings and vestments, they soar above the studio, peering down at bales of river-willow twigs, reeds, cattails, dried flowers, native grasses and feathery fronds. He lists onion skins, corn husks, clay, and 24K gold leaf as some of his favorite art supplies. Armando continues the traditions of previous generations of *campesinos,* who made objects of great beauty and imagination from anything at hand, and the reverberations of previous craftsmen are present in every detail of this warm, welcoming studio. "When I enter my studio space, I feel I am in *my* space," Armando says, "and it is a familiar and comfortable feeling." ◯

ARTIST Nancy Anderson

It is hard not to fall under the spell of Nancy Anderson's creations. And once you've visited her studio/workroom, resistance is futile. Music is playing. The dogs, Chester and Lamb Chop, welcome you inside. Nancy and her talented assistants are busy at their worktables and jeweler's benches. Strands of red chili lights are tangled around weathered, sun-bleached rustic furnishings and displays. Purple walls, green walls, orange walls, flashes of silver, precious stones, faceted beads, get-happy toy sheriff's badges, and chunks of beach glass— everything has a place. As Nancy says, "It's a dance."

This all-encompassing world is where Nancy conducts the business of Sweetbird Studio, although she laughingly resists calling it "the office." The reasons are obvious. Although this joyous, hard-working studio includes all the expected practical necessities, they're surrounded by billowing tableaux of rampant relics, memorabilia, comfy thrift-shop furniture, exotic carpets, and inexplicable random discoveries.

Nancy happily debunks the theory that, to create, one must have a perfect space. "Give up that thought *now*!" she says. "The perfect space only exists in your dreams. I say: Just create! Let it happen in your basement, that less-than-optimal rental, your shower, your kitchen table. Just do it." These are hard-earned words of wisdom from Nancy, whose studios have not always been ideal (a five-foot [1.5 m] -square space in a basement, alongside a furnace, for example).

Before she began working side-by-side with her assistants and fellow jewelers, Nancy questioned if she could share such an intimate personal work space with others, but now she exclaims, "I would be lost without my daily muses—and the love and creativity we share."

How about visitors to the studio? "I always welcome visitors!" Nancy says. "I revel in someone seeing the beauty in what I might take for granted. Their visits to my personal space are a reminder that what I do matters." One memorable day, a man wandered into the studio, looked around, and compared it to a "voodoo shop in New Orleans" he had once seen. Little did he know he was giving Nancy a huge compliment; it was one of those "we can't make this stuff up" experiences that still brings a smile and a hoot of laughter.

> "There is my life in my studio ... and then there is me. It is all part of the same thing. Me. The studio. We are one. Selling your artwork —it's like wearing your soul on your sleeve. It is the most personal thing I could ever do for a living."
>
> — **NANCY ANDERSON**

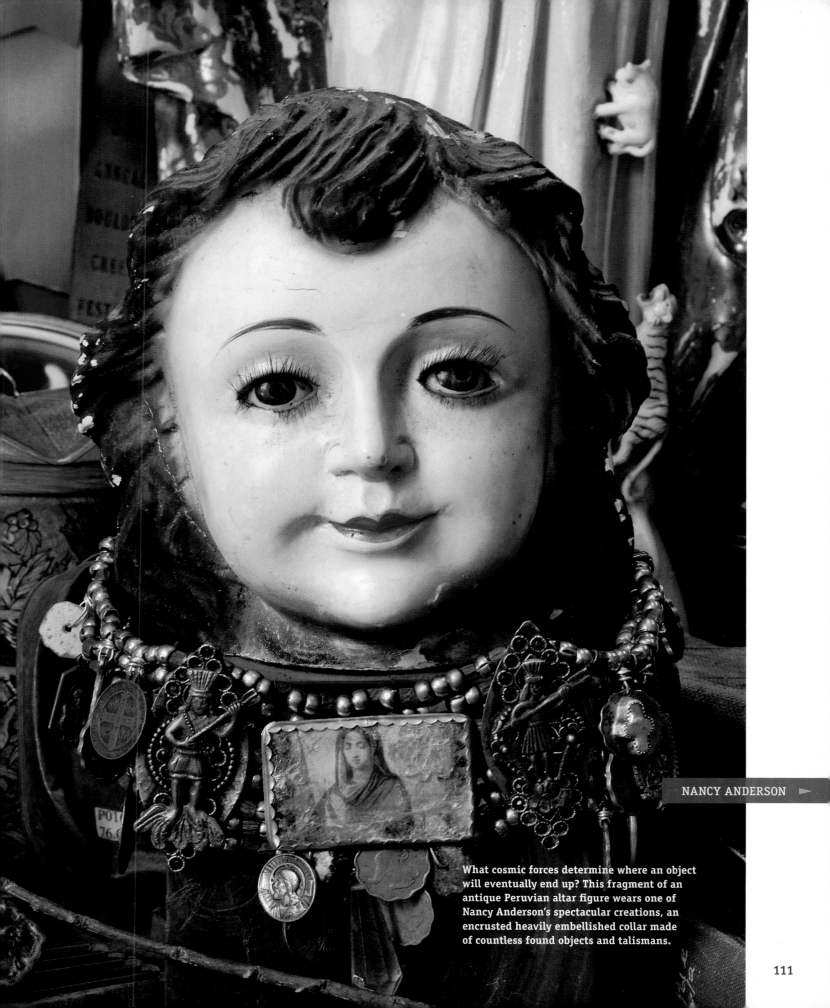

What cosmic forces determine where an object will eventually end up? This fragment of an antique Peruvian altar figure wears one of Nancy Anderson's spectacular creations, an encrusted heavily embellished collar made of countless found objects and talismans.

Nancy is an advocate of the "Just Show Up!" school of creative thought, "Don't *try* to be wonderful and talented," she cautions. She has learned (and earned) the value of just arriving at her jeweler's bench, "scooting things around," and allowing good ideas to emerge and develop. The surroundings in the studio constantly welcome and cheer her, and they prompt new ideas … for example, the new ring designs displayed below.

Why be ordinary? Nancy includes something extra with each design, often a secret sly quote or design detail inside the ring that only the wearer will know about. Her lifelong work as a jeweler, her so-called "hobby gone mad" brings her intense joy, and that spills over to her product line, her life, and her environment. She wouldn't have it any other way. In a perfect example of "I can't stop myself," even her product displays are made from found objects and provide the ideal backdrop for her original jewelry designs.

Nancy laughs off the idea that her work space was ever created around some specific plan and credits evolution and serendipity as the guiding forces behind her studio. She expresses the hope that everyone who enters the space will respond to the heart of the work. One of her prized possessions is a notebook full of thank-you notes, emails, cards, and drawings from her customers.

NANCY ANDERSON ▶

113

Part gypsy cave, part full-tilt fiesta, Nancy's work space spills over with her collage papers, castings, old books, and her collection of tin. Each rustic armoire, wooden packing crate, and vintage suitcase spills the goods, and she defines her space as functional—gritty, not pretty. A corner of her office, behind the main work room, provides an insight into what makes Nancy tick. A crowded bookcase is chock-a-block with used books, old magazines, and almanacs, collected for their offbeat subject matter. An out-of-date calendar hangs on the wall, providing strong colorful graphics. A tall, one-of-a-kind, cracked-mosaic lamp sheds light on Lamb Chop, one of two faithful studio dogs that never leave Nancy's side. ◉

"Hang in there for the surprise."

— **NANCY ANDERSON**

ORIENTATION
Following the Squiggly Line
GPS 42.086078° latitude
−73.619767° longitude

In 1953, Bob Blechman sat down at his kitchen table and wrote and illustrated his first book, *Juggler of Our Lady: a Medieval Legend,* and he's been busy ever since. Ten-hour days in the studio, seven days a week, are not unusual for Bob. When you drive down his country lane, past rolling pastures and the mailbox, you eventually come to his compact studio building, and his reason for spending so much time there becomes obvious. Park the car by the large maple tree and come to the entry door, inset with vintage stained glass. Bob lists books, toys, and stained-glass windows as some of his favorite things, and he's made room for all of these inside his inviting and engaging studio. The well-loved collections are arranged and edited with the careful eye of an inveterate art director; nothing is cluttered or chaotic.

Long ago, the building was a seldom-visited antique shop doomed to obsolescence because no one traveled the quiet country road except farm animals. It's a story that would probably be a perfect topic for one of Bob's sly animated films. Luckily, the Blechman family came along and rehabilitated the property, and the little shop was fully renovated into the studio. Eventually, two more wings were added for storage and a full bath, along with other updates.

After a long career in the arts, Bob has a confident compass about nearly everything. "My criteria for studio space is the same for my work," he says. "I satisfy my primary client— me—and invariably that is what others like, too."

He reveals that his studio is more his home than his actual home, while confessing that many of his best ideas occur when he is away from his work space—often in bed. "Then I grab a pencil and write something down for the next day," he says. Sometimes, music becomes part of the stimulation inside the studio—"strong stuff, like Stravinsky or Shostakovich"—but usually he works in silence, surrounded by the sounds of his country environment.

R.O. BLECHMAN ▶

"My studio inspires me. It's very visual."

— **R.O. BLECHMAN**

R.O. BLECHMAN ▶

Bob describes the "necessity" of having a studio: "I need a separate space, a space that says 'work,' the way a dining room or bedroom has a specific function." It's hard to argue with this successful formula; Bob's creative output in the past fifty-plus years has been remarkable. His *New Yorker* covers, illustrated books, ad campaigns, a Museum of Modern Art retrospective of his animated films, one-man exhibits here and abroad—all this is from a man who is always fully engaged, chasing the next great idea.

This well-organized space features a main studio with several workstations, plenty of storage and flat files, a wall-to-wall expanse of art and visual reference books, complete with a rolling library ladder, a seating area for guests or contemplation, and an outer office for additional storage. There is no mistaking the bucolic country setting; windows provide a glimpse of all four seasons, just outside.

An arrangement of small toy airplanes is staged on a windowsill, and a vintage display card of plastic combs echoes the jewel-like colors of the stained glass windows and doors. Whether all of these like-colored objects were brought together intentionally or the harmony was pure kismet, the outcome is the same. Every visual element in the room hums in accord, resulting in an ultra-personal work space. ◉

"Years ago—maybe thirty—I bought a collection of toy airplanes but had no place to display them. Now they fit in comfortably with the décor. I tend to be fussy about the overall appearance of my studio, so if something seems out of place, no matter how much I love it, I don't display it."

— R.O. BLECHMAN

ORIENTATION
Palimpsest

GPS 41.326580° latitude
−73.435020° longitude

"I could live with raw umber and black for the rest of my life. It has infinite possibilities, grad-ations, subtleties—it has tonal variations that are very beautiful."

— **FRED OTNES,** *Collage Paintings*

This statement, about his personal art aesthetic, also applies to Fred Otnes' home and studio environ-ment. Furnishings are classic and handsome, selected with an art director's eye: black leather, bold graphic accents, and bibelots, white walls, lots of dramatic windows—nothing extraneous. And best of all: artwork by Otnes. A lot of it.

When I met Fred, he was just about to send a huge body of work to the Reece Gallery in New York City for an exhibition, so the timing of my visit was fortuitous. "If you had come a week later, the place would have been empty," he says. Throughout the living and working areas, large groups of framed collage paintings awaited transport. It was a bonanza.

Just beyond the open-plan living room is one of Fred's studios, a well-lit area furnished with a large worktable on casters and incorporating open storage for collage materials and works in progress. Wall-to-wall book shelves nearby

FRED OTNES ▶

hold his reference library, as well as small props gathered for their intrinsic value to his more-dimensional, "structural work." Otnes, a seminal collage artist, who literally transformed the graphic illustration scene of the '70s and '80s before turning to fine art, is known for his distinctive, lushly layered surfaces. Elegant, engaging accumulations of photographic and archival images, selected with a master's eye, are then adhered, scraped off, overpainted, distressed and then skillfully and selectively obscured. His goal, to create a complex surface full of subtle elements that gradually engage the viewer, is reflected in the collection of potential collage elements spread out on the worktable, forming a compost of endless possibilities.

Inspired and provoked by images from master artists such as Caravaggio, Titian, and Piero della Francesca, Fred is just as likely to be energized by African art or Art Brut. Each glimpse of an admired work of art can suggest a possible path to take—perhaps an approach to composition or the use of a particular color. He's not averse to picking up leftovers, his previous failed works lurking in his storage drawers, and transforming them by painting over or sanding the surface. He also reveals that sometimes an utterly blank canvas or piece of paper is the ultimate motivator.

A compact room nearby has a lightbox stand for viewing slides and a storage unit for keeping track of completed work, publications, reproductions, and files. The view from the living room, into the nearby studio, provides a still life of Fred's immaculate and organized work space. Easily accessible and available, it is a meticulous reflection of his design sense, a study in white, beige, gray, black, and brown.

"Most people think of art in terms of the tools you use—they have categories in their minds related to the instruments the artist uses rather than the action. They think if you're using a pencil or a pen, you're making a drawing, and when you pick up a brush, a drawing becomes a painting. But in reality it's the same damn thing. If you pick up an airbrush, its still drawing. If you're doing a collage figure, you use the same mental process to determine how you're going to represent the body. It's an image out of your head going onto a surface."

— **FRED OTNES,** *Collage Paintings*

FRED OTNES ▶

Fred's "other studio," in a separate building, is a no-nonsense space with plenty of large worktables and storage for paints, adhesives, solvents, and materials. Several wooden flat files, positioned throughout the space, keep papers, collage fodder, and reference materials organized and easily accessible. His etching press, a studio essential he has had for decades, stands at the ready. Recently, he has been using the press to create a series of lushly colored, highly detailed prints based on exotic Indian textiles. An array of the colorful prints, fanned out for maximum impact, creates a fascinating display on a worktable, which is topped with a vintage articulated mannequin hand from Fred's collection of wooden objects.

The frankly utilitarian mood of this work space, along with the stylish and elegant ambience of the studio adjacent to the living room, are two expressions of the intuitive and masterful work ethic of Fred Otnes. The artist, who admits he appreciates handsome things, has created a lifetime of work that bears his strong signature but never reverts to formula. ◉

ARTIST Sarah Blodgett

She not only has a real studio—a contemporary, well-organized and light-filled work space/gallery —she also has a home studio in her vintage country farmhouse. Ask Sarah Blodgett about her favorite studio, and she is apt to answer: "It's wherever I happen to be." This photographer, who goes everywhere and anywhere to get the shot, is always on the move. A homebody infected with wanderlust, she handles every phase of professional photography with aplomb, including portraits, product shots, interiors, art prints, landscapes, and more. A selection of her large framed prints reveals her passion for nature and her family and friends. Creating a tableaux of natural objects, which she has staged throughout her home and studio, is a continuing mania, and Sarah has recently turned her camera on the artifacts, capturing the microscopic variety of pods, seeds, sticks, dried mushrooms, ferns, feathers, and rocks.

At the top of a steep staircase in the old farmhouse, wall-to-wall shelves provide plenty of storage space for her photographic archives, binders, notebooks, quirky antique frames and props, a vast collection of vintage photos, and family snapshots, which are tucked and displayed throughout. A mood of coziness prevails, and a big overstuffed couch in front of the window welcomes visitors to plop down and stay awhile … even though Sarah's camera bags and tripod are right at the front door, ready for the next assignment. ◉

"When I enter my studio, I feel like a song has just begun. I never know which song it will be, but I love music and try to get something out of every tune I hear. Sometimes I get a broken record or some heavy metal … but never Muzak."

— **SARAH BLODGETT**

ARTIST Pamela Armas

ORIENTATION Xanadu, the Casbah, and the Whole 9 Yards
GPS 34.520885° latitude
−106.240579° longitude

Far better than slipping down the rabbit hole with Alice, a visit to Pamela Armas' studio will transport you to faraway lands without ever having to pack a bag. Inside the 20,000-square-foot (6,096 m²) repurposed automotive garage is a warren of increasingly fascinating and overflowing art spaces, some of them designed as working studios for Pamela, others providing a suitable exotic environment for all of her collections. Outside the curvaceous metal entry gates, the southwestern landscape is arid, windswept, and spare. Inside, every inch is filled with lavish colors, silky tassels, an international bazaar of patterns and motifs, bolts of both silky and textured imported fabrics, flashes of sequins and beads, and much more.

Pamela's travels throughout the year not only take her to fascinating locales to buy new wares, they also bring her to trade shows, where she promotes and sells to kindred collectors and artists. Her buying excursions are akin to a traveling gypsy caravan of experiences, cultures, and discoveries that become a "studio at large." In fact, the name of her business is Treasures of the Gypsy.

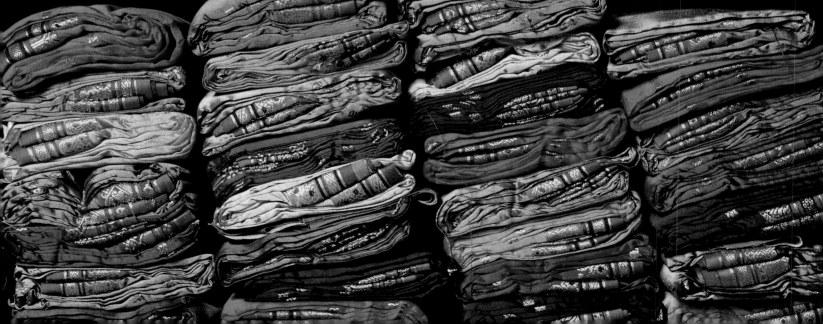

A spacious worktable is set up in the front gallery for cutting and folding bolts of fabrics, and the vast selection is displayed according to color groups. Storage is a key visual component throughout the space, and a huge variety of imported cabinets, armoires, chests, and "things with drawers" provides additional fascination. The contents of each drawer deliver glimpses into different cultures. Lighting is designed to provide efficient illumination of the work spaces as well as dramatic theatrical effects in the display areas. "It's important for me to be surrounded by color and beautiful things from my overseas travels and personal collections," Pamela says. "My studio spaces are not only organized, functional, and efficient, they're also showcases for art and treasures."

> "I am on the road doing several shows during the year. Coming home is so exciting for me. I fall in love with everything all over again. My entire building is an extension and expression of my art."
>
> — **PAMELA ARMAS**

PAMELA ARMAS ▶

Pamela has various studio spaces set up throughout the overall building, each bearing a different title: "Treasures," "Hope," and "Nature." In each studio, she keeps a small journal, in which she notes the positive and negative aspects of the space, and she continually thinks of ways to refine and perfect all the studios. One of her stitched works of art, featuring innumerable amulets, charms, milagros, and talismans, appears on an easel in a large sun-filled room dedicated to working with paper, collage, and stamping. A spacious worktable is surrounded by ample storage, and a wall-to-wall bookcase holds her art research library. Tucked among the books is a family of handmade art dolls, some by Pamela, others by her favorite doll artists.

A consummate collector, her studios overflow with her various manias, all integrated in artful niches and compelling displays. Even childhood mementoes—small dolls, marbles, stamps, rocks—find their way into the exotic mix. Another studio is dedicated to her design work, fabric and fiber art, and contemporary cloth dolls. A third area, at the rear of the warehouse, is for painting, gluing, and found objects, a so-called "messy space" that is still remarkably organized, artful, and staged … à la Pamela.

Inside the sewing studio, a king's ransom in beads, buttons, and embellishments is stored inside efficient, white cabinets. Once the doors are opened, the treasures within—smooth teak Asian amulets, twinkling cut-crystal beads, colorful hanks of fibrous eyelash trimming, burnished amber knobs, and trimmings and edgings from almost every culture—offer endless color and surface ideas and stimulation. The sewing machine is in place, ready for any sudden inspiration, and a wise, knowing handmade doll sits nearby as a silent witness to the strong flow of creativity here.

PAMELA ARMAS

"Being in my studio strokes my imagination and is enriching to my soul. I feel most alive surrounded by the beauty, richness, and opulence—it fills me with possibilities."

— **PAMELA ARMAS**

ARTIST Jamie Purinton

ORIENTATION
From the Ground ... Up
GPS 42.098564° latitude
-73.545564° longitude

As a landscape architect, Jamie Purinton not only finds inspiration in her sturdily constructed and ultra-personal studio, with its drafting table, files, and reference materials, she also finds inspiration in her outdoor environment, which she constantly uses as a laboratory and testing ground for ideas.

I first discovered Jamie's gardens and studio during a local garden tour and was taken with her story of how she wanted to make the most of her narrow wooded lot, which leads down to a small scenic lake. Inspired by similar lots near Montreal and in the Finger Lakes wine region of New York, Jamie wanted to create "an edible landscape," where she could grab a bite to eat while wandering through the gardens, orchards, and mini-vineyards on a summer day (and pick a bouquet of flowers for the dinner table, in the bargain). All of this, and more, has come true in this magical outdoor setting, which is visible from the large windows over her drafting table.

Jamie partnered with her husband, Tad, to build this timbered studio extension to their home. Over a year-long period of construction, the overall plan changed and morphed, as new ideas for materials and construction details were considered. "Drawings, photographs, and books have accumulated over the years, pushing my storage needs," Jamie explains. "Because I have recently become passionate about playing bluegrass with other musicians, my studio sometimes becomes a social space, so I am often rearranging the furniture to make it work for four to five musicians."

As her design work evolved, Jamie increasingly focused on ecology and sustainability, and the eighteenth-century landscape etchings on the walls of the studio were eventually replaced by artwork done by friends and natural collectables such as wasp nests and dried branches.

"I love being in my studio. After twenty years of being a landscape architect, I find that anxiety still accompanies the process. I need to see the accumulation of work I have completed, to help give me the confidence to start new projects when confronted with a blank sheet of vellum on my drafting table."

— **JAMIE PURINTON**

Far more than just a decorative outdoor structure, Jamie's potting shed provides an additional creative work space, right in the heart of the garden, as well as an enticing and welcoming place to sit with a glass of iced tea on a warm day. The small structure, which was salvaged from a neighboring overgrown lot, was moved to the garden and rehabilitated with a mix of repurposed found objects and artful touches. An old door from a roadhouse restaurant was refitted for the entryway, vintage garden tools cover the rough-sawn wooden walls, and thick braids of Jamie's homegrown garlic hang from the rafters. On either side of the door, vintage garden spades, painted with expressive faces by mixed-media artist Bill Wilson, serve as unique sentries. During fair weather, the compact, welcoming space serves as an additional studio, where Jamie can be surrounded by the sights, sounds, and aromas that she loves, while being only steps from her vegetable and cutting gardens.

The gardens overflow with bounty—Jamie and Tad share a passion for growing fruits and vegetables, always trying new crops and mowing patterns—and Jamie's artful design sense assures that their outdoor environment is also full of visual fascination. A bonanza of rusted horseshoes studs the open-wire garden fencing. Old-fashioned tea pots perch on posts marking the spot where chamomile is planted. Curvaceous, old iron bedsteads have been repurposed as entry gates, at the top and bottom of the vegetable garden plots. Throughout the garden are places to sit, contemplate, brainstorm, sketch, and design, making the entire environment a "studio of the great outdoors."

"I feel grateful to have this life and this space."

— **JAMIE PURINTON**

JAMIE PURINTON ▶

Jamie's indoor studio is every bit as personal as her outdoor environment and has a prevailing made-by-hand feeling that is cozy and welcoming, rain or shine. An old library catalog file houses project photographs and slides, and steel milk pails from a local dairy barn are used for rolled drawings and plans. Office supplies are kept in old wooden boxes, and pencils, sorted according to color, are kept in terra cotta flower pots. Books are arranged by key subjects, and folders of images of benches, streams, bridges, and paths are carefully organized—the artist describes a propensity for mulching her open spaces with paperwork and drawings. Jamie lists inspiring, resourceful, and comfortable as the three most important components of a successful studio, and she is likely to spend an average of twelve to fourteen hours here each day. The outdoors continually calls to her. "I go back and forth between the studio and the garden and the shed," Jamie says. "This keeps me grounded in the hands-on aspect of my work."

She and Tad continue to expand their gardens, so they can put more and more food away for year-round consumption. "I love our home and our gardens and know that they reflect our values and lifestyle," Jamie says. "The value of growing our own food, encouraging wildlife, organic gardening practices, even saving rain water from the roof … all of these things create a positive experience and are part of my approach to my work."

Jamie describes the perfect studio as being both a nurturing nest and a place to experiment. She observes that it should be less a place for *showing* work and more a place for *doing* work—"not a performance space, but a jamming band room!"

"Having a studio and working gardens makes a big difference to me. Both give me confidence, inspiration, experience, and knowledge. Seeing the plants each day and throughout the year inspires me to come up with new combinations of colors, textures, and forms. It feeds my passion for the work I do."

— **JAMIE PURINTON**

Laurie Beth Zuckerman

ORIENTATION
Membranes of Memory
GPS 40.574397° latitude
−105.069435° longitude

In direct opposition to the idea that a studio should be behind closed doors, in a designated specific area, Laurie Zuckerman's philosophy is to consider her entire house as her studio. This premise not only works, it absolutely radiates. Entering Laurie's home for the first time, one is instantly captivated and engaged by room-after-room arrangements of altars and memory jugs. Her laser vision applies to gathering the artifacts necessary to create the artwork, determining the placement of each important visual aspect, and the way in which she incorporates her artwork into her living area. It all works perfectly. "Because my artwork revolves around making home-altar installations, being able to set them up *in situ* makes practical sense," Laurie explains.

From the viewer's perspective, practicality has very little to do with the rampant, amazing, intensely personal artwork displayed throughout Laurie's home. Rather, entering her home is a rare opportunity to spend time communing with countless hand-selected artifacts arranged into a tableaux of stirring significance and radiant meaning.

When she first moved into her home, Laurie was confident that the basement would provide sufficient space for her work and her collections. That space, which has since been declared "the epicenter," is literally filled with elements for new installations that are spread out amid an ever-accumulating compost of more, better, and different finds. Of necessity, "the overflow spilled onto the upstairs dining table and floor."

To visitors, the light and airy dining room seems art-directed with a curator's eye to present Laurie's impressive memory jugs, which are displayed on a vintage rustic table surrounded by a family of different-but-kindred wooden

"I adore my rustic antique harvest table from southern Virginia. I can work on it freely without worrying about it getting scratched … it is already plenty distressed."

— **LAURIE ZUCKERMAN**

LAURIE ZUCKERMAN ▶

chairs. This artful, orderly room often becomes "jam-packed with art projects lining the wall" and is used as an off-season display for countless cactus plants … and, of course, as a family dining room. "We include everything," Laurie says, "making space to squeeze in our various projects as well as our meals."

Laurie, who prefers the solitude and convenience of working at home, also has a separate "clean space," a light-filled office with a desk, computer, and a view of the backyard, turtle pond, and bird feeders. She shares this space with her cat and two parrots, and she's placed a well-loved, green antique rocker in the office, so her husband "can sit and visit." Here, she does her art marketing, digital photography, and business communications. Three of her larger home altars also share the space. She describes her criteria for a successful work space as, "Light, warmth, and proximity to my altars, my husband, and my animals." It's all here. And more.

A living room tableau hums with the combined fascinations of many cultures and includes ethnic textiles, thriving cactus, an impressive array of Laurie's memory jugs, and a herd of treasured, folk-art animal figures from around the globe. A rustic vessel holds a grouping of eccentric flamingoes—each bird, cast in cement and painted in the exuberant way of self-taught instinctive artists, is just another example of Laurie's ability to find singular, soulful works of art to express her personal aesthetic. Her own artwork blends seamlessly with her collections and favorite significant belongings, and she refers to her home as "my showroom, my gallery, my museum."

One of Laurie's majestic memory jugs, created in remembrance of her mother, commands a special place in the living room, amid a tableau of other significant collections. Small items that might find their way into future memory jugs are stored in antique wooden boxes with multiple drawers and a nearby tower of cigar boxes.

"My entire house is an expression of my artistic creations. Every aspect of my work is made from antiques and vintage possessions I have collected from places I have lived or traveled."

— LAURIE ZUCKERMAN

LAURIE ZUCKERMAN ▶

Mother of Pearl Memory Jug,
by Laurie Zuckerman
21" × 10" (53.3 × 25.4 cm)

Shallow cardboard flats are also repurposed for storage and as sorting bins for found objects, separated according to color. Her doll shrine, staged inside a magnificent rustic sideboard, is one of many large altars throughout her home, and Laurie is constantly adding to it. The storage drawers of her altars slide open to reveal real life things, such as stationery, office supplies, paperwork, and clothing.

Space is an important issue for this artist, who was once laughingly accused by a friend of having a fear of empty spaces. "You need space to make things," Laurie says emphatically. "Space to think. There is never enough space to make new work, view work in progress, or store old work." She describes the pace of her work as "fiendish" and insists on beginning a project only if she has sufficient time to work in a nonstop, driven manner. As she readies the work for a new exhibition, she is frequently overwhelmed by the enormity of the piles of unmade stuff in the workroom downstairs and the dining room, but eventually everything coalesces according to her plan.

"Yes, I love my house being filled with my artwork, made from my collections. It is always a feast for my soul. I am the only person in the world who fully understands my work and appreciates it. That fact makes me feel sad and isolated at the same time—but then the work compensates by making me feel at home and totally contented."

"This moment of transcendence makes every collected object, be it a matchbox or a martyr's fingernail, valuable. Every collected item is, to some extent, a totem."

— **PHILIPP BLOM,** *To Have and To Hold*

ARTIST **Michael deMeng**

I might be in the midst of painting … but *then* I need to drill something." Michael deMeng discusses the heroic goal of keeping separate work areas in his studio for separate tasks but then laughingly says, "Next thing I know, things are everywhere." Notorious for leaving open jars of paint and tubes of glue while rushing off in pursuit of completing the next great idea, Michael describes his manner of working as "sporadic." He speculates that a helper in the studio—someone who could put things back where they belong—would be a wonderful addition. However, the helper would have to be invisible and unobtrusive. And anyway, having things organized would probably just throw him off his game. So, scratch organization off the list, and let's just go straight to inspiration.

There is plenty of it in Michael's studio, a place he describes as "all work." For all his self-deprecating jokes about his lack of order, Michael still claims to be able to find anything in the studio at any time. "It is amazing; with all the heaps of stuff, I can usually find the tiniest thing based on my memory of where I had it last," he says.

This frankly utilitarian space is all-business—the business of being Michael. He insists on the space being flexible and available for any art exploration that might occur to him on any given day. Orderliness and cleanliness are not the key criteria—it's all about working with any new ideas and impulses, full-tilt. For example, Michael describes a possible scenario in which he might decide to—oh, say—throw an open jar of gesso into the air and let it splatter everywhere. In the end, having the permission to be fully expressive in his studio is his top priority. (And if he ever gets around to trying the gesso-in-the-air thing, he'll let us know.)

MICHAEL DEMENG

151

> "Often they are salvage operations, rescue missions designed to save from extinction something that others would not stoop to pick up or hesitate to throw away."
>
> — **PHILIPP BLOM,** *To Have and To Hold*

Michael prizes the feeling of being focused while in his studio and values having a work space designed specifically for doing his art. "I feel like I need to get to work and do something important. No messing around," he says. His emphasis on a sacred space that is his alone—"It is my special place"—causes him to marvel at the flexibility of artists who come to study with him in a temporary workshop environment. "I have never been the type to make art in random locations," he reveals, stating that any potential studio would require getting used to. In the meantime, don't expect Michael to pull up to the kitchen table or find a work space in the garage next to the garden hose and begin work. He insists on having his dedicated art space, with all of its imperfections.

In fact, he says, the disarray in his studio can often be a helpful thing, when it comes to his distinctive way of working. Random events happen. He describes a continuing scenario of moving things about and discovering a long-out-of-sight object, which miraculously provides the perfect something in a current assemblage.

"Out of chaos comes order ...
or at least something cool."

— **MICHAEL DEMENG**

MICHAEL DEMENG ▶

"Best to avoid the temptation," says Michael, explaining his insistence on keeping his own treasured collections away from the studio because he might be tempted to alter and use them in his assemblage work. He describes his studio as utilitarian and confesses that his space is a reflection of how his mind works. "I am seemingly disorganized, but within that disorganization is order," he says. His hammer may not be in the toolbox … but at least he knows where to find it—under an old dashboard.

Printers' trays are useful for corralling small items and keeping them visible, rather than hidden away in drawers. An old upright steamer trunk is a recent acquisition, its already-full drawers and storage space with hangers awaiting some new assignment. "I'll come up with something," Michael says, "maybe a place to dry out my snakeskins."

Visitors in the studio? If pets count as visitors, the answer is "fine." Otherwise, visits are not generally encouraged, because Michael is usually on-task and preoccupied, busily conducting his love/hate relationship with the place. If things are going well—lovely. If not, watch out. His least-favorite time in the studio is the never-never-land between the completion of one project and the beginning of the next. The necessity to clear the decks, reorganize, and clean up adds to the frustration. "The ghosts of the previous piece of art can be a problem for future projects," he explains. Sooner or later, his work environment adjusts to his latest brainstorm—"My space evolves as I work on a specific piece of art."—and then peace is restored.

The power tools hum, and the racket of the drill drowns out the ringing phone. A new idea is afoot … and all is well in the world according to deMeng. ○

Judy Wilkenfeld's studio in Sydney, Australia, might seem remote, but her stories about her studio, her artwork, and her strong ties to her art colleagues reveal a story of vital connectedness. One of the most compelling displays in her main studio work area, a rustic ladder strung with more than 100 vintage children's shoes, is a case in point. Judy expressed an interest in buying any antique children's shoes that others were willing to part with and posted a notice on her blog. She was gifted with shoes that arrived from everywhere. "They poured in from all over the world and still do," she says. Other restored ladders throughout the studio display ethnic textiles, embroidery, and fragments of exotic garments and banners, all presented against the dramatic dark-brown walls of her studio.

Judy invited a consultant in feng shui to work with her to establish the most auspicious placement of the major fixtures in her main studio, the aptly named "clean space." The overall space includes the studio, a drilling and metalworking space, a painting area, and a storage and packing facility. She says that her own personal evolution, including newly discovered techniques and manias for new materials, is the single, most-important factor in guiding the changes that take place in the studio. Known for her mixed-media Visual Anthologies, comprised of endless artifacts and significant talismans, Judy's studio overflows with her special collections, which are stored in handsome antique wooden cabinets, glass jars, wooden sewing-machine drawers, specialized, repurposed containers —and one Depression-era Australian food safe. Not only a jaw-dropping, commanding visual accessory, the restored steel cabinet rotates to reveal a total of twenty-eight drawers of all sizes. Antique dolls are housed in glass containers or in wooden drafting drawers, and Judy's goal is to have all of her encyclopedic collections readily available to speed up the creative process.

"To communicate the message of tolerance and understanding is imperative in my pieces. What better place than my studio to remind me of my message?"

— JUDY WILKENFELD

JUDY WILKENFELD ▶

Judy's desk is located in the center of her studio and is completely surrounded by visual displays of her collections of art materials and artifacts. Massive Thai teak bowls in various shapes are kept on her desk for storing essential tools, and antique Chinese wooden rice storage containers house her fabric collections.

When working on a commissioned piece, Judy requires absolute concentration, and she immerses herself in interviews as well as intensive research. She often feels she is entering a time warp, in which a past culture, environment, or society commands her current reality and takes over. By creating a personal and thoughtfully organized studio environment, she is able to easily transition to any mindset that is needed to create and sustain her work.

Every time Judy enters her studio, her gaze is drawn to an array of photographs of children who perished in the Holocaust. These past lives serve as Judy's inspiration, and when she is seated at her worktable, they serve as watchful eyes, urging her on.

"The desk I work on is an antique Australian country kitchen table; it has traveled from house to house with me. Formerly our family's kitchen table, it has a rustic appeal, and, over time, my children have carved their names into it, drawn on it, and manhandled it. To me, it represents home and comfort … important elements to bring into my studio."

— **JUDY WILKENFELD**

JUDY WILKENFELD ▶

Although Judy's studio is the place in which she constructs and assembles her Visual Anthologies, her self-described "global studio" is where she hunts and tracks down the visual elements needed to create her highly detailed and personal work. In fact, the hunting and gathering is a significant part of her creative process, and each of her favorite places for collecting becomes a far-flung studio at large. "I bring the world inside my studio, and there the items remain until needed," Judy explains.

One special collection, a gathering tribe of old fascinating suitcases, commanded too much space in her main studio, so they were moved upstairs, where they have become a collective installation. Each suitcase either contains a Visual Anthologies piece or will become a housing for a future work.

Judy takes us along on a road trip, revealing some of her favorite haunts for collecting and gathering. Happily cluttered thrift shops, eccentric merchandise stacked to the rafters, and cavernous used-book stores are part of her regular route. An artist who is intent on finding the perfect

"… but the attic and the cellar are tied to the temporality of the past, and they scramble the past into a simultaneous order which memory is invited to rearrange: heaven and hell, tool and ornament, ancestor and heir, decay and preservation."

— **SUSAN STEWART,** *On Longing*

JUDY WILKENFELD ▶

Sparkling Chandeliers, all vintage & antique.
Profusely adorned...with an emphasis on the rare & unique.
Hand-picked, then invited from around the world,
Precious Present comes standard...every contour, every curl.
Healing, Inspiring, Mystical & True;
Future Treasure their stoic, humble gift to you.
Timeless, with a story, its crystal with a past...
Each and every one, crafted from the heart.
Its a Wonderous gift to embellish the soul,
Deeper Beauty warms the heart, whether young or old!!!

visual element to tell each story—"My commissioned pieces require absolute concentration."—she has been known to drive hours to find a specific color of book cloth or track down a far-flung recommendation or resource for old manuscripts.

Also too numerous to mention: Judy's favorite places for finding her artifacts. Whether scouring the countryside in her homeland of Australia or turning up fascinating finds during her travels in the United States, Judy is the consummate collector. As she considers a current commission, or merely speculates what might be needed in the future, her gathering process is a direct extension of her creative process. Far from shopping, her collecting expeditions are vital to the work she does in her calm, quiet, personal studio space.

In Judy's hands, everyday objects are used to create visual narrations of past lives and cultures. She never knows where she might find the ideal thing, and there is no sure formula for finding the perfect object. Her travels might take her to a favorite decorative shabby-chic shop glittering with chandelier parts and then to a retro-thrift shop full of cultural icons that spill out onto the sidewalk and command the roof of the owner's car as additional display space. Every resource provides a different possibility, every stop is part of the continuing chase. The outside world provides the inner workings for Judy's work, and every new hunt extends the boundaries of her constantly expanding studio-at-large.

"I have many special collections, too many to name."

— **JUDY WILKENFELD**

JUDY WILKENFELD ►

No trip to Judy's studio would be complete without an exploration of one of her exquisite Visual Anthologies©, an assemblage of memories, meant to be slowly examined, explored, regarded, and considered and constructed from the most humble of materials: worn book parts, found photos, bisque dolls, feathery cheesecloth, vintage book pages, buttons, and a carefully saved children's game piece. The collective elements hum in harmony, the result of long, sometimes-inexplicable journeys from far-flung places, through Judy's studio, and now out into the world. ⊙

"The souvenir is not simply an object appearing out of context, an object from the past incongruously surviving in the present; rather, its function is to envelop the present within its past. Souvenirs are magical objects because of this transformation."

— **SUSAN STEWART,** *On Longing*

ARTIST Johnnie Meier

ORIENTATION
Roadside Warrior

GPS 36.206228° latitude
–105.960757° longitude

At first, it's hard to grasp the full significance of Johnnie Meier's self-described Classical Gas Museum. Located on a snaking scenic road leading to Taos, New Mexico, this expansive, captivating compound reveals itself gradually and includes a museum of restored roadside treasures, an indoor/outdoor work space spilling over with tools and specialized equipment, and an eclectic outdoor storage and display area full of items awaiting restoration, replete with flowering fruit trees. I recommend that visitors begin by having a frosty root beer from the antique ice chest on the front porch of the museum. The small wooden building, a quintessential vintage gas station, is deceptively modest, but, inside, it is literally aglow with neon product signs and logos, expertly restored gas pumps, meticulously displayed and arranged oil cans, vintage automotive toys, tin signs, jukebox selector boxes, and at least one shiny, black manual typewriter. Best of all, there is the resident genius behind all of this, Johnnie Meier.

A lot about the highways and byways of America has changed, but spending some time in Johnnie's environment brings it back with a smile, even if you are too young to grasp the nostalgia. "Stuff comes into my workshop distressed, broken, discarded, and unappreciated," he says. "When the completed stuff leaves the workshop, it is renewed, recovered, and ready to once again be appreciated."

Looking at the rows of stately, pristine, formerly rusted gas pumps, with their colorful crowning illuminated toppers, the significance of Johnnie's mastery becomes obvious. An offer to "come and see the workshop" was eagerly accepted, and I was given a tour of one of the most fascinating, specialized and personal work spaces ever.

More than a decade ago, Johnnie began acquiring specific equipment and tools to help him achieve this mastery. These include a sandblasting cabinet, an HVLP paint system, and an exhaustive inventory of hardware items, which he buys by the hundreds. Storage solutions in the workshop, although varied and no-nonsense, are visually fascinating—a length of pegboard displaying an impressive rainbow of colorful screwdrivers, for example, with the Southwestern afternoon sun poking through. A wall of old post office boxes provides convenient compartments for filing, and old coffee cans are hard to beat.

This craftsman and restoration expert declares that the key component to an efficient work space is convenience and easy access to his tools. He wistfully remarks that a "self-cleaning" work space would be the answer to a dream but also confesses: "The dirtier you get, the more you accomplish. If I emerge from my workshop with sawdust in my hair, grease on my forehead, a rip in my jeans, and paint on my hands, then I must have had a good day!" (Clearly, the grunge and silt of accomplishment trumps any mythically tidy studio, and I suspect many artists in this book feel the same way.)

JOHNNIE MEIER

Peering into the main area of the workshop reveals a sense of industrious, ongoing work, while pending projects wait in the wings. Johnnie prefers filling his work space with future projects.

"One builds a relationship and a sense of comfort having a future project around," he says. "It may sit in the workshop for six months while I work on something else, but while it is waiting, I am absorbing it." Johnnie prefers to have several projects underway at once, as a way of keeping motivated and enthused all day. The large work area opens to the outdoors, where a nearby shaded picnic table serves as an extra workbench. And, of course, there is an extensive outdoor area, where upcoming projects awaiting renewal are displayed. Visitors stop by daily, captivated by the view from the road of the countless old gas pumps in various states of decline, vintage autos with fins, and displays of defunct license plates, rusted horseshoes, and other widgets. Somehow, it all looks like a magical kingdom, one of those places that exudes good vibes and the potential for fascination.

Standing inside the museum, the whole place warmly aglow with illuminated ad signs and colorful neon, it is easy to connect with Johnnie's assessment that he's doing something significant, lasting, and important. He compares his restoration work to Zen-like tasks such as carrying water or chopping wood, emphasizing that "the work is the thing." For visitors fortunate enough to spend some time in this singular environment, the rewards and awareness are endless. And an ice-cold root beer makes the experience just about perfect. ⊙

> "One builds a relationship and a sense of comfort having a future project around."
>
> **— JOHNNIE MEIER**

INDEX OF ARTISTS

Oxidized horseshoes take a rustic chair in Johnnie Meier's storage area.

Photographic family archives in Sarah Blodgett's home studio.

Rustic tools cover the walls in Jamie Purinton's garden shed and outdoor studio.

Faye Anderson
sparkle_plenty@comcast.net

Nancy Anderson
Sweetbird Studio
4949 N. Broadway, Ste. 116
Boulder, CO 80304
303-440-9891
www.sweetbirdstudio.com
info@SweetbirdStudio.com

Pamela Armas
P.O. Box 748
Mountainair, New Mexico 87036
GypsyTreasures@cs.com

R.O. Blechman
205 Tompkins Road
Ancram, NY 12502
ro@roblechman.com

Lyn Bleiler
4277 NDCBU
Taos, NM 87571
Lyn.bleiler@yahoo.com

Sarah S. Blodgett ~ Photographer
518-755-4933
www.Sarahblodgett.com
sarah@sarahblodgett.com

Sas Colby
2817 Ellsworth Street
Berkeley, CA 94705
510-841-8827
510-908-2514 (mobile)
www.sascolby.com
sas@sascolby.com

Michael deMeng
www.michaeldemeng.com
assemblage@michaeldemeng.com
www.michaeldemeng.blogspot.com

Lisa Hoffman
lisahmixedmedia@gmail.com

Ellen Kochansky
1237 Mile Creek Road
Pickens, SC 29671
864-868-4250
www.ekochansky.com

Keith LoBue—Jeweler, Artisan, Stuffsmith
www.lobue-art.com

Armando López
P.O. Box 169
Abiquiu, NM 87510
505-685-4585
www.armandoLópez.com
Armando@armandoLópez.com

Johnnie Meier
johnniev@roadsideculture.com

Terri Moore
Blue Door Studio
P.O. Box 86
Lakeville, CT 06039
bluedoorstudio@earthlink.net

Tracy V. Moore
P.O. Box 3329
Renton, WA 98056
www.zettiology.com
www.teeshamoore.com

Glittering exotic light fixtures dangle from an overhead grid in Pamela Armas' "Treasures" studio.

Maria Consuelo Moya
studiomcm@yahoo.com

Linda O'Brien
www.burntofferings.com
http://burntofferings.typepad.com

Opie O'Brien
www.burntofferings.com
http://burntofferings.typepad.com

Fred Otnes
c/o The Reece Galleries, Inc.
24 West 57th Street, Ste. 304
New York, NY 10019
212-333-5830
www.reecegalleries.com

Lynne Perrella
www.LKPerrella.com
LKPerrella@AOL.com

Jamie Purinton
Jamie Purinton Landscape Architect
and Gardener

Pollock-Krasner House and Study Center
830 Fireplace Road
East Hampton, NY 11937
631-324-4929
www.pkhouse.org

Judi Riesch
jjriesch@AOL.com
www.itsmysite.com/judiriesch

Monica Riffe
Fort Collins, CO
monriffe@hotmail.com

Bee Shay
bee.shay@hotmail.com
www.beeshay.typepad.com

Steven Sorman
www.stevensorman.com

Pam Sussman
8340 Beech Avenue
Munster, IN 46321
219-923-4240
PamSussman@AOL.com

Michelle Ward
www.michelleward.typepad.com
grnpep@optonline.net

Bill Wilson
Ghent, NY

Judy Wilkenfeld
Visual Anthologies©
http://redvelvetcreations.blogspot.com/
judy@wilkenfeld.com.au
http://visualanthologies.blogspot.com/

Melissa Zink
The Parks Gallery
127 Bent Street
Taos, NM 87571
www.parksgallery.com

Laurie Beth Zuckerman
iconARTe: altars, memory jugs, and
shrine photography
970-482-5589
lauriezuckerman.blogspot.com
zucky@qwest.net

About the Author

Lynne Kendall Perrella is a mixed-media artist, author, and workshop instructor. For more information and inspiration, please visit: www.lkperrella.com

Acknowledgments

What a super opportunity! I have always wanted to write a book about studios, and this was my chance to not only visit studios here in the Hudson Valley, but also to travel throughout the Northeast and Southwest. My photographer, Sarah Blodgett, the best traveling buddy ever, captured every detail and nuance. I also received excellent contributed photos from several artists. My editor Mary Ann Hall kept the project on track and provided great coaching and clarity, as ever. Thanks to all of the artists who provided such fascinating insights into how they feel about their studios and creative work spaces.

Without a doubt, one of the highlights of this project was another chance to visit the studio of Melissa Zink, of Taos, New Mexico. Several years ago, I had my first encounter with her work in an exhibit titled "The Lost Libraries" at The Parks Gallery. I wrote her a letter in care of the gallery expressing my admiration, and to my great surprise she wrote back. This initiated our correspondences that eventually lead to visits to her studio over several years. My latest visit was during the summer of 2008 when Sarah and I documented her work space and spent time talking about a wealth of mutual fascinations. It was a rare opportunity to "come inside" and observe the studio of an admired artist I discovered by chance; and then came to know as a dear friend and creative mentor.

With thanks to Melissa for her generous hospitality and unwavering zeal for getting into the studio and chasing ideas, no matter what.

For Donald Westlake (July 12, 1933–December 31, 2008) This book is lovingly dedicated to Don Westlake—stellar friend, mystery author extraordinaire, Oscar-nominated screenwriter, raconteur, country neighbor, city slicker, teller-of-stories, and maker-of-mischief.